The Tyranny of Gun Control

Edited by
Jacob G. Hornberger
and
Richard M. Ebeling

Fairfax, Virginia

ISBN 1-890687-00-6 (hb.) — ISBN 0-9640447-7-3 (pbk.)
Copyright © 1997

The Future of Freedom Foundation
11350 Random Hills Road, Suite 800
Fairfax, VA 22030

Library of Congress
Catalog Card Number 97-060309

Printed in the United States of America

Contents

Preface v
by Jacob G. Hornberger

Introduction ix
by Richard M. Ebeling

1. Loving Your Country and
    Hating Your Government 1
    by Jacob G. Hornberger

2. Will You Be Safer If Guns Are Banned? 7
    by Jarret Wollstein

3. The Assault-Weapons Scam 15
    by James Bovard

4. Gun Control, Patriotism, and
    Civil Disobedience 25
    by Jacob G. Hornberger

5. Real Independence Day:
    The Meaning of the Second Amendment 31
    by Richard J. Davis, D.D.S.

6. What the Second Amendment Means 35
    by Sheldon Richman

7. The Right to Life Equals
    the Right to Possess Firearms 39
    by Sheldon Richman

8. Gun Control: A Historical Perspective 45
    by Benedict D. LaRosa

9. The Nazi Mind-Set in America 55
    by Jacob G. Hornberger

10. Citizen Exploitation Isn't New 65
  by John L. Egolf Jr.

11. Waco and the Cult of the Omnipotent State 69
  by Jacob G. Hornberger

12. Terrorism—Public and Private 73
  by Jacob G. Hornberger

13. The Oklahoma Tragedy and the Mass Media 79
  by Richard M. Ebeling

14. The Hypocritical War on Terrorism 85
  by James Bovard

About the Authors 91

About the Publisher 93

Preface

Our American ancestors instituted the most unusual society in history. They refused to permit such things as income taxation, welfare, regulation, Social Security, Medicare, Medicaid, public schooling, and gun control. And no one can honestly dispute that even with the exception of slavery and the Civil War nineteenth-century Americans lived in the most free, prosperous, and harmonious society in history.

Twentieth-century Americans have rejected the principles of freedom of their ancestors. Believing that the socialistic welfare state would provide them with a "safety net" of governmental security, they traded the liberty bequeathed to them by their ancestors for the paternalistic state. Thus, they adopted all of the things to which their ancestors had said No: income taxation, welfare, regulation, Social Security, Medicare, Medicaid, public schooling, and gun control.

The result of the socialistic welfare state, including the governmental wars on poverty, drugs, bigotry, and illiteracy, is a society in which there is ever-increasing drug abuse; violent crime; gang wars; inner-city decay; deteriorating public schools; class and race warfare; ever-increasing levels of taxation; government assaults against innocent men, women, and children; highway robbery by the police against innocent Americans; invasions of privacy; and the rise of militia groups all over the country who wish to protect themselves from all of this.

An ever-growing number of Americans are now questioning the tenets of the socialistic welfare state. They are recognizing that an overwhelming number of societal problems are attributable, either directly or indirectly, to the socialistic welfare state that has characterized most of twentieth-century America.

Thus, more and more people are calling for the dismantling, not the reform, of such agencies as the Internal Revenue Service; the Bureau of Alcohol, Tobacco and Firearms; the Drug Enforcement

Administration; and the Departments of Housing and Urban Development, Health and Human Services, Education, Energy, and Commerce. Some have even suggested that, with the end of the Cold War, the CIA should be abolished and the military-industrial complex drastically downsized. An increasing number of Americans are finally recognizing what their Founding Fathers realized: that the biggest threat to the safety and well-being of a citizenry lies not with some foreign government but rather with its own government.

The problem is that U.S. government officials, as well as the recipients of governmental largess, are not about to meekly surrender the benefits they reap from the paternalistic state. America's domestic wars, the socialistic welfare state, and the desire for foreign empire have produced tens of thousands of people who not only are hooked on the governmental junk but also honestly believe that they have a right to it. Moreover, all too many government agencies take the provocative position that "national security" would be jeopardized if their part of the government were abolished rather than simply reformed.

If the American people continue moving in a direction of restoring liberty and harmony to our country, and if U.S. government officials continue to resist the trend, the tensions in this country are certain to rise.

What will be the outcome? Who will give in? We automatically assume that the government will, but recent events are not encouraging: the gassing of innocent women and children at Waco, Texas; the killing of an innocent woman at Ruby Ridge, Idaho; the CIA's participation in tortures and murders in Latin America, not to mention their tampering with election results; and the long-time cover-up of radiation and drug experiments by U.S. government officials against innocent Americans.

If the American people decide to recapture the principles of liberty of their ancestors, it is impossible to predict the reaction of U.S. government officials, especially if they view the dismantling of the socialistic welfare state as a threat to "national security." But lessons can be drawn from recent U.S. military incursions into other countries. The first thing U.S. government officials do after an invasion is disarm the citizenry through warrantless searches and seizures. They know that a disarmed citizenry is always an obedient citizenry. If we are to preserve the option of leading the world out of the socialistic morass, it is imperative that the American citizenry remain well armed. The best assurance of a compliant governmental servant is a well-armed citizen-master. U.S. government officials must not be tempted to do to American citizens what they have done to foreigners.

People have the moral right to own property, including guns. They have a right to protect themselves from murderers, rapists, and robbers. Most important, as America's Founding Fathers emphasized so often, people have the fundamental right to arm themselves in order to protect themselves from public tyrants whose official conduct threatens to become worse than that of private murderers, rapists, and robbers.

—*Jacob G. Hornberger*
President
The Future of Freedom Foundation

Introduction

The Second Amendment to the United States Constitution reads:

> A well regulated Militia, being necessary to the security of a free State, the right of the people to keep and bear Arms, shall not be infringed.

For the Founding Fathers and for the Americans of the newly formed United States, the right to self-defense was a principle that followed naturally from their belief in individual liberty. Rights preceded governments; they were not given to people by government. "We hold these Truths to self-evident," the Founders proclaimed in the Declaration of Independence, "that all Men are Created equal, that they are endowed by their Creator with certain unalienable Rights, that among these are Life, Liberty, and the Pursuit of Happiness. . . ." They went on to say, "That to secure these Rights, Governments are instituted among Men, deriving their just Powers from the Consent of the Governed. . . ."

Governments, however, could be tyrannical; they could try to deny the right to life and liberty possessed by the people. "[Whenever] any Form of Government becomes destructive of these Ends," the Founders said, "it is the Right of the People to alter or to abolish it, and to institute new Government. . . ." Most of the Declaration is an enumeration of the abuses and tyrannical acts the signers of the Declaration argued the British government had committed against the settlers and British subjects of the original thirteen colonies. Their own government, in other words, had violated their civil, political, and economic liberties.

As the signers expressed it, among the many violations of the people's freedom, the king had "erected a Multitude of new Offices, and sent hither Swarms of Officers to harass our People, and eat out their Substance." He had instituted legislation "For cutting off our

Trade with all Parts of the World: For imposing Taxes on us without our Consent. . . ." And when the people had finally chosen to take up arms in defense of their rights as free individuals, the signers said the king had

> plundered our Seas, ravaged our Coasts, burnt our towns, and destroyed the Lives of our People. He is, at this Time, transporting large Armies of foreign Mercenaries to complete the works of Death, Desolation, and Tyranny, already begun with circumstances of Cruelty and Perfidy, scarcely paralleled in the most barbarous Ages, and totally unworthy the Head of a civilized Nation.

After listing all of their grievances against the British Crown, they solemnly pledged to each other "our lives, our Fortunes, and our sacred Honor" in the struggle for winning independence and freedom for the people of the United States of America.

The right to bear arms, therefore, was not based only on a need for hunting food or warding off the attack of the savages of the forests. No, it was a right that was considered essential as a protection against the tyranny of one's own government. The signers of the Declaration did not believe that armed resistance was in itself a good thing or that it should be resorted to capriciously. But they did believe that it was an ultimate right when the abuses of a government had finally gone beyond repair or reform. Indeed, it was the fact that the colonists of America were armed and familiar with the use of firearms that made it possible for them to stand up for their rights and win their freedom in the American Revolution. After the war was won and the debates were joined in the 1780s over the ratification of the Constitution, both Federalists and Anti-Federalists agreed on the importance of the right to bear arms.

In *Federalist* No. 29, Alexander Hamilton said:

> Little more can reasonably be aimed at, with respect to the people at large, than to have them properly armed and equipped. . . . [If] circumstances should at any time oblige the government to form an army of any magnitude, that army can never be formidable to the liberties of the people while there is a large body of citizens, little, if at all, inferior to them in discipline and the use of arms, who stand ready to defend their own rights and those of their fellow-citizens.

And in *Federalist* No. 46, James Madison pointed out:

Notwithstanding the military establishments in the several
kingdoms of Europe, which are carried as far as the public
resources will bear, the governments are afraid to trust the
people with arms.

Anti-Federalist John De Witt pointed out:

It is asserted by the most respectable writers upon government,
that a well regulated militia, composed of the yeomanry of the
country, have ever been considered as the bulwark of a free
people. Tyrants have never placed any confidence on a militia
composed of freemen.

Richard Henry Lee, another leading Anti-Federalist, declared
that to preserve liberty, "it is essential that the whole body of the
people always possess arms, and be taught alike, especially when
young, how to use them."

To ensure the liberties of the people, Patrick Henry insisted:
"The great object is, that every man be armed. . . . Everyone who is
able may have a gun."

But gun ownership in the name of having a means of last
recourse for preserving liberty would be hollow if government,
especially the federal government, controlled and directed their use.
Said Patrick Henry:

Are we at last brought to such a humiliating and debasing
degradation, that we cannot be trusted with arms for our own
defense? Where is the difference between having our arms in
our own possession and under our own direction, and having
them under the management of Congress? If our defense is the
real object of having those arms, in whose hands can they be
trusted with more propriety, or equal safety, as in our own
hands?

Tench Coxe explained the purpose of the Second Amendment
in the Philadelphia *Federal Gazette*.

As civil rulers, not having their duty to the people duly before
them, may attempt to tyrannize, and as the military forces

which must be occasionally raised to defend our country, might pervert their power to the injury of their fellow-citizens, the people are confirmed by the next article [the Second Amendment] in their right to keep and bear their private arms.

And the New York convention that ratified the U.S. Constitution stated: "That the people have a right to keep and bear arms; that a well regulated militia, including the body of the people capable of bearing arms, is the proper, natural, and safe defence of a free state."

What did "a well regulated militia" mean? It is fairly clear that in the minds of most of the discussants in these debates, it meant local, voluntary groups of the people—members of the respective communities around the country—who would form associations for the purpose of mastering the proper uses of firearms and for organized training in military arts suitable for defense against either a foreign invader or a domestic authority that might attempt to usurp power and infringe on the people's freedom.

After Waco and Ruby Ridge and numerous other less publicized cases of brutal and unjustified use of force against American citizens by the government, can anyone say that the fears and arguments of the Founding Fathers are any less valid now than when the passages quoted above were originally penned more than 200 years ago? Government is, and always has been, the greatest criminal threat to the peaceful members of society. Meant, in the best of circumstances, to serve as the protector of people's rights, the great problem of government has always been to devise a successful answer to the question: Who guards the guardians? The American Founding Fathers, thoughtful and knowledgeable thinkers that they were, concluded that the best means was a written constitution in which the limited powers of the national government would be clearly enumerated, with the powers of the government divided among three branches, and a supporting Bill of Rights that emphasized in no uncertain terms that there were certain individual liberties that the federal government must not intrude upon. And to reinforce the primacy of individual rights and the clear, planned limitations on the federal government, the Founding Fathers concluded the Bill of Rights with the Ninth and Tenth Amendments, which state, respectively: "The enumeration in the Constitution, of certain rights, shall not be construed to deny or disparage others retained by the people," and "The powers not delegated to the United States by the Constitution, nor prohibited by it to the States, are reserved to the States respectively, or to the people."

But what if, in spite of these most determined institutional restraints on the government, that government were to expand its power and compass trespassing upon the freedom of the people? Well ... that is what the Second Amendment to the Constitution was meant to provide—a final recourse for the people to protect their life, liberty, and property from the grasping, controlling, and taxing hand of the federal government. Gun control—the disarming of the American people—would take away this final line of defense for the preservation of liberty. This, more than anything else, is why we should be concerned with opposing the tyranny of gun control. It not only leaves the innocent, peaceful, law-abiding citizen unarmed before the common criminal or organized gang that may attempt to plunder his property or threaten physical harm and injury to himself or his family. It will confiscate the last, real weapon the people have to defend themselves against the potential plunder or physical harm that could befall them at the hands of their own government, especially in times such as our own, when that government has overreached the limits placed upon it in the Constitution and continues to massively overreach them.

The Future of Freedom Foundation was founded in 1989 to champion the cause of individual freedom. In a century and in a world in which the individual has been brutalized, enslaved, and murdered in vast numbers by governments, the Future of Freedom Foundation takes as its working premise that tyranny in all its forms must be opposed and that wherever freedom has been lost, an uncompromising case must be made for its rebirth. For a long time now, the government of the United States has been attempting to steal that precious right of self-defense reflected in the wording and in the spirit of the Second Amendment. Most of the essays in *The Tyranny of Gun Control* were originally published in the Foundation's monthly journal, *Freedom Daily*. Together, they are meant to present a thorough and uncompromisingly principled case for the individual's right to own firearms and against any and all restraints, regulations, or prohibitions on gun ownership.

Why is it important? Because on the issue of the people's right to privately own and bear arms without government control and regulation may ultimately rest the future of freedom in America.

—Richard M. Ebeling
Vice President of Academic Affairs
The Future of Freedom Foundation

1

Loving Your Country and Hating Your Government

by Jacob G. Hornberger

During his first term in office, President Clinton condemned Americans who exposed and criticized wrongdoing by the U.S. government. The president said: "There's nothing patriotic about hating your government or pretending you can hate your government but love your country."

Let us examine the implications of the president's claim.

In the 1930s and throughout World War II, there was a small group of German citizens who sacrificed their lives resisting the Nazi regime. They believed that the true patriot was the person who lived his life according to a certain set of moral principles. When one's own government violated those principles, it was the duty of the patriot, these Germans believed, to resist.

Adolf Hitler and the Nazi regime, on the other hand, believed that the real patriot was the citizen who supported his government, especially in times of crisis and war. The traitors, in their eyes, were the Germans who opposed the Nazi government, especially after the war had begun.

The story of the small number of Germans who resisted the Nazi regime is told in a recent book—*An Honourable Defeat* (1994) by Anton Gill. Gill points out that by the end of the war, most of the German resisters had been identified by the Gestapo and murdered. He says:

That this is the story of a defeat none will doubt. Some will dispute that it was an honourable one. It is certainly not the story of a failure. Against terrible odds and in appalling circumstances a small group of people kept the spirit of German integrity alive, and with it the elusive spirit of humanity. We should all be grateful to them for that.

What would President Clinton say about these resisters? Undoubtedly, he would call them troublemaking traitors to the Nazi regime. After all, the president would ask, how could these people claim to love their country and, at the same time, claim to hate the Nazi government? The real patriot, the president would say, was the German citizen who loved his country and, therefore, his government. As President Clinton would have said to the German resisters, "There's nothing patriotic about hating your government or pretending you can hate your government but love your country."

What about the British colonists living in American in 1776? They certainly had no love for their government. When we celebrate the Fourth of July, it is easy to forget the real implications of what happened during the fight for independence. It is important to remember that George Washington, Thomas Jefferson, James Madison, John Adams, John Hancock, and the rest were not American citizens when the Declaration of Independence was signed. They were as British as you and I are American. And they hated the philosophy and policies of King George—taxation, economic regulation, immigration controls, trade restrictions, and so forth.

The colonists were violent men. They did everything they could to kill the soldiers who fought on the side of their own government. On the other hand, British soldiers did all they could to bring death to their fellow citizens. As we celebrate the Fourth of July each year with our fireworks and picnics, we tend to forget that real people with real families were deliberately killed on both sides of the conflict.

Were the colonists patriots? Certainly the British government did not think so. Nathan Hale (who regretted that he had but one life to give for *his country*) was hanged because he was a traitor to *his government*. If the rebellion had failed, there is no doubt that the signers of the Declaration of Independence would have all been put to death by their own government officials—for treason.

What would be President Clinton's position with respect to the War for Independence? On the surface, he would, of course, sing the praises of America's Founding Fathers and American Independence Day. But this would only mask a deep-seated resentment against the colonists. What gave them the right to take up arms against their own government? Clinton would ask. They had no right to resist tyranny by force. They should have continued to plead and lobby for political representation in the Parliament. William Jefferson Clinton would have said to Thomas Jefferson: "There's nothing patriotic about hating your government or pretending you can hate your government but love your country."

A hundred and sixty years ago, a small band of Mexican citizens took up arms against their own government. Despite popular misconceptions, many of the rebels at the Alamo, Goliad, and San Jacinto were not Americans. They were not Texans. They were Mexican citizens. They had pledged allegiance to the flag of the Republic of Mexico. Why did they engage in violent acts against their own government officials? Because they hated the regulations and the taxation that the Mexican president, Santa Anna, was imposing on them.

Were the rebels patriots or traitors? Their position was that patriotism meant devotion to ideas like liberty and property. They believed that the real patriot—the person who loves freedom—resists his own government when his government becomes destructive of fundamental rights. Of course, Santa Anna took the position that these Mexicans were, instead, traitors to their government and their country.

Unfortunately, President Clinton would share Santa Anna's perspective. By becoming Mexican citizens, he would say, the colonists had pledged to support their government officials, even when the latter were taxing and regulating them. It was wrong, President Clinton would claim, for the Mexican colonists to have considered themselves patriots. After all, "There's nothing patriotic about hating your government or pretending you can hate your government but love your country."

Actually, the president's mind-set is the same as that held by tyrants throughout history. In the mind of the ruler, the government and the country are one and the same. The citizen who has the temerity to expose and criticize wrongdoing by his own government is, ipso facto, a traitor to his country. The citizen who supports his government's conduct, no matter how evil or destructive—and who doesn't ask uncomfortable questions—is a real "loyalist."

Consider the deaths at Ruby Ridge and Waco. At Ruby Ridge, U.S. government officials persuaded Randy Weaver to commit a crime—selling them a shotgun that was one-fourth of an inch too short. After a U.S. marshal was killed in a subsequent shootout at the Weaver home, the FBI put out the following order: Do not demand a

3

surrender; do not try to arrest; we do not want a jury trial here; instead, take them out; kill them all; shoot them until they are dead; teach them that no one kills a federal official, not even in self-defense; but make it look good by ensuring that the victims are armed. So, after having shot Weaver's 14-year-old son in the back, the feds shot Weaver's wife ,Vicki, in the head. Fortunately, they were unsuccessful in killing Weaver and were humiliated by the jury at Weaver's trial.

Was that the end of it? Oh, no. The FBI then engaged in a cover-up of this Latin American-style death squad's conduct. FBI officials falsified and destroyed documents, perjured themselves, conspired to obstruct justice, and refused to obey orders from the U.S. Attorney's office. In their minds, the FBI is an independent, national, patriotic police force (like the Gestapo and the KGB) that can punish citizens with impunity, without the time and trouble of a trial, and without having to answer to anyone.

Has any federal official been brought to trial for murder, perjury, conspiracy, or obstruction of justice? Of course not. The feds have tried to buy justice by paying Weaver and his children $3.1 million. The money, of course, came from American taxpayers, not those who committed the crimes. What happens if a taxpayer refuses to pay his taxes by claiming that he did not commit the crimes? They kill him for "resisting arrest." All of this is what Justice Department employees term "justice."

Of course, the federal attitude towards what happened at Waco is exactly the same. Federal officials secured a search warrant from a federal judge under a perjured affidavit. They decided against a low-profile search of the premises and against apprehending the Branch Davidian leader—David Koresh—outside the compound. They needed a bigger "splash" for upcoming budget hearings.

So, the feds planned a high-profile raid that they termed "Showtime." But "Showtime" did not quite work out as planned, for several federal officials lost their lives in the raid. And the deaths of those officials ultimately sealed the fate of the Branch Davidians. No one can ever accuse U.S. government officials of playing "softball"— "kill a federal official, and you won't have to worry about a trial or anything else."

The recent movie *Braveheart* shows that political attitudes toward defiant citizenry have not changed much over the centuries. The attitude of King Edward and his minions toward the Scottish people many centuries ago was quite similar to that of President Clinton and his underlings toward American dissidents. King Edward had Scottish people raped, tortured, and hanged for failing to

4

pay proper deference to His Royalty; and His Majesty never had even one ounce of remorse.

Is President Clinton's and the Democrats' attitude toward American dissidents any different? It is true that FBI and BATF officials did not rape Vicki Weaver before they killed her—and that they did not rape the Branch Davidian women before they gassed and burned them. And we should give credit where credit is due. But is there *any remorse whatsoever* over the political killings of innocent people?

In the recent congressional hearings on Waco, the Democrats, led by Rep. Charles Schumer, made a grand spectacle of being concerned about child abuse in the Branch Davidian compound. The implication was this: "Our concern for the Branch Davidian children is evidenced by our concern about possible child abuse in the compound."

What nonsense! The truth is that the Democrats did not care one bit for the Branch Davidian children or for any other individual who was gassed and burned alive in the compound. How do we know this? Because, again, *there is not one bit of remorse for the loss of life at Waco*. The Democratic attitude is instead the same as that held by the FBI and the BATF: These were white-trash, weird people, and so it is no big deal that they—and their children—died.

Moreover, the Democrats feel that since David Koresh might have been engaged in child abuse, federal officials had the right to kill him without a trial (despite the fact that he is innocent until proven guilty)—and, in the process, to kill the other hundred people who were not even accused of child abuse (including the dead children).

And the Republicans? They are similar to the nobles in *Braveheart*. The nobles would pontificate on the virtues of freedom and the importance of principle. But as soon as the king offered them money and lands, they would betray all of their ideals. Is this not the case with Republicans? Republicans are notorious for talking the libertarian talk—even now calling themselves libertarians—but they are totally unable to walk the libertarian walk. Offer them votes or campaign contributions or a congressional chairmanship, and they sell their souls very easily.

Unfortunately, during the recent hearings on Waco, the Republicans were so concerned with upholding their law-and-order image that they treated the FBI and BATF with kid gloves. The Republicans think that if they expose police murders, conspiracies, perjuries, and cover-ups, this might hamper law enforcement in the future. Thus, Republicans did not even try to secure the appointment of an independent counsel to investigate and prosecute the FBI and BATF death-squad activity. More important, the Republicans failed to obtain any reasonable assurance that the death squads would not be used again under "appropriate" circumstances.

What was so uplifting about *Braveheart* was that small band of Scottish men, led by William Wallace, who loved their country and hated their government. Like many who had come before them—and who have come after them—they refused to compromise their principles.

President Clinton was wrong when he said: "There's nothing patriotic about hating your government or pretending you can hate your government but love your country." Throughout history, there have been courageous and honorable individuals—patriots—who have loved their country and hated their government. And, unfortunately, throughout history, there have also been weak and cowardly people—traitors—who have loved and supported the tyranny of their own government.

It is to the patriots—not the traitors—that we owe Magna Carta, the Petition of Right, habeas corpus, the presumption of innocence, trial by jury, due process of law, private property, and so many other aspects of human freedom. It is the patriots—not the traitors—who have remained steadfast for principles of right, even when it meant incurring the wrath and retribution of their own government officials. And it will be the patriots—not the traitors—who ultimately triumph in America and end our government of the pestilence that pervades it—so that, once again, American patriots will love their country and not hate their government.

This essay originally appeared in the October 1995 issue of Freedom Daily, *published by The Future of Freedom Foundation.*

2

Will You Be Safer If Guns Are Banned?

by Jarret Wollstein

Violence is out of control, and guns are a major cause. This is a belief many Americans now share. This belief is fueling a nationwide movement that could result in a total prohibition on private gun ownership in the near future.

Private ownership of guns is being banned one step at a time. The recently enacted Brady Bill mandates a national five-day waiting period and background check for all handgun purchases. Maryland has just passed a law that requires a state license for any handgun purchase and limits purchases to one per month. And President Clinton has banned the importation of most foreign-made semiautomatic rifles.

On February 28, 1994, Treasury Secretary Lloyd Bentsen announced that several 12-gauge semiautomatic shotguns were being reclassified in the same category as machine guns. The Bureau of Alcohol, Tobacco and Firearms simultaneously announced that they would trace the owners of 18,000 of these shotguns and order them to be fingerprinted and to register their guns with the ATF within 30 days—or face ten years' imprisonment and a $250,000 fine.

On the same day that semiautomatic shotguns were reclassified, Sen. Howard Metzenbaum introduced legislation that would require all handgun owners to get a federal license, pass a safety test, and register their weapons with police.

Sen. Daniel Patrick Moynihan has proposed legislation that would raise the tax on some ammunition up to 10,000 percent. The price of a single box of Winchester 9-millimeter hollow-tipped cartridges would increase to $15,000.

Would banning guns reduce crime?

According to recent polls, most Americans now support gun licensing as a way to reduce crime. Crime has certainly been increasing—particularly violent crime. Between 1960 and 1980, robberies nationwide increased by 300 percent. In the same period, both the number of handguns and the national murder rate doubled.

But is the proliferation of guns the cause of violence or a response to violence? As Daniel D. Polsby of Northwestern University demonstrated in his article "The False Promise of Gun Control," which appeared in the March 1994 issue of *The Atlantic Monthly*, there is no evidence that firearms cause violence:

> If firearms increased violence and crime, then rates of spousal homicide would have skyrocketed, because the stock of privately owned handguns has increased rapidly since the mid-1960s. But . . . rates of spousal homicide in the years 1976 to 1985 fell.
>
> If firearms increased violence and crime, the crime rate should have increased throughout the 1980s, while the national stock of privately owned handguns increased by more than a million units in every year of the decade. It did not.
>
> If firearms increased violence and crime, Florida's murder rate should not have been falling since the introduction, seven years ago, of a law that makes it easier for ordinary citizens to get permits to carry concealed handguns. Yet the murder rate has remained the same or fallen every year since the law was enacted. . . .

Paradoxically, although firearms do not increase crime and violence, gun-control laws do! Throughout the United States, when strict gun-control laws are passed, crime and violence get worse.

Since 1976, it's been illegal in Washington, D.C., to own any handguns or to keep any type of gun fully assembled in your home. Nevertheless, Washington, D.C., has among the highest murder rates in the nation. New York City has had a virtual ban on firearms since 1967, yet it also ranks among the most dangerous places in the country to live. In both New York and Washington, violent criminals can easily obtain machine guns and other deadly weapons on the streets within minutes.

Why does increased violence go hand-in-hand with gun control laws? The reason is that disarmed people make easy targets.

If an armed criminal attacks you on the street or in your home, you cannot afford to wait 30 minutes, 20 minutes, or even 10 minutes for police to arrive—assuming you even get the chance to call police and they respond. Ten minutes is more than enough time for a thug to rob you, rape you, shoot you, or cripple you for life. If the government takes away your guns, you are at the criminal's mercy.

Self-defense does work. According to Morgan Reynolds of Texas A&M University, armed citizens deter one million crimes each year. "In 98 percent of the cases, simply brandishing the weapon or firing a warning shot is sufficient deterrence."

In Florida, forcible rapes sharply declined in Orlando and other cities after police trained women to use guns.

During the Los Angeles riots, armed Korean merchants successfully defended their stores from looters after police retreated. Many undefended stores were burned to the ground.

In Los Angeles, many neighborhoods were protected from rampaging mobs only by residents blockading their streets and brandishing guns. If guns had been illegal, their homes would have been looted and burned, and many would have been raped or killed.

Why the rise in crime and violence?

If armed self-defense works, and if gun ownership is increasing, why does violent crime continue to escalate?

Of course there are many reasons, including the breakdown of families, violence generated by drug prohibition, and the lack of jobs for young adults, particularly in the inner city. But as economist Paul Craig Roberts points out, a major reason is that outside of our homes, we are already a disarmed society.

In most of the United States, it is a crime to carry a gun on the street, so most people do not. And criminals know it. Not surprisingly, 87 percent of all violent crimes occur outside the home.

Another major reason why crime is increasing is that crime pays, and in our tax-ridden, regulation-crushed economy, many people cannot economically survive through low-end jobs. As Professor Polsby points out, "The income that offenders can earn in the world of crime, as compared with the world of work, all too often makes crime appear to be the better choice."

In Washington, D.C., it costs $7,000 in city fees to open a pushcart. In California, up to eighty federal and state licenses are required to open a small business. In New York, a medallion to operate a taxicab costs $150,000. More than 700 occupations in the United States require a government license. Throughout the country, church soup kitchens for the homeless are being closed by departments of health. No wonder so many people turn to crime and violence to survive.

Banning guns solves none of these problems. And "tough crime laws" also will not help. The risk of being caught if you are a criminal is extremely low: nationwide, only 1.2 percent of all burglaries result in a conviction.

But we can protect ourselves and deter crime by owning guns and knowing how to use them. Professors James Wright and Peter Rossi's landmark study for the Department of Justice found that 85 percent of felons serving time in prison agreed that "smart criminals" will try to find out whether their potential victim is armed before attacking him. Fifty-three percent did not commit a crime, for fear that the victim was armed. And 60 percent felt that most criminals feared armed citizens more than police. (Wright and Rossi, *Armed and Considered Dangerous: A Survey of Felons and Their Firearms,* 1986.)

There are many dramatic examples of how Americans have used guns to protect themselves and stop criminals. Here is one that I particularly like:

Until recently it was legal to carry loaded guns in public in Texas. Twelve years ago, when a holdup man in Dallas tried to rob a bank, he got a deadly surprise. No fewer than two bank customers and one teller pulled out guns and shot him dead. Not surprisingly, the bank-robbery rate in Dallas has been a fraction of what it is in other large cities.

The initial effect of stringent new gun control in the United States has been exactly the opposite of what was intended. It has produced a huge surge in gun purchases.

Dean Barber, business columnist for the *Birmingham News*, reports, "In the gun trade, of which Birmingham is a national center, there is an incredible run on guns and ammunition." Panic buying is now the norm "because of the perception that you will not be able to buy the gun of your choice in the not-so-distant future." (Llewellyn Rockwell Jr., "Bull market in weapons," the *Washington Times*, January 13, 1994.)

Millions of Americans want to be able to defend their homes, their families, and themselves, and they will break the law to do it. As David B. Kopel explains in his book *The Sumurai, the Mountie, and the Cowboy*:

> American gun owners—even more than their counterparts in other countries—will massively resist any form of gun control. . . . Registration laws for semiautomatic firearms in

Denver and Boston have achieved a 1 percent compliance rate. It is evident that New York City's near-prohibition is not voluntarily obeyed; estimates of the number of illegal guns in the city range from seven hundred thousand to three million. The New York state commissioner of prisons testified that if 1 percent of illegal handgun owners in New York City were caught, tried, and sent to prison for a year, the state prison system would collapse.

Gun prohibition threatens your safety and your life. Prohibition will make it much more difficult for you to defend yourself and your family from predators. Prohibition will create a violent black market dominated by criminal gangs. And prohibition will result in many police assaults and murders of innocent Americans.

Gun control laws will make our streets safer for violent criminals. With an estimated 200–700 million guns now in the United States, an unpoliceable 12,000 miles of borders and coastline, and the world's largest stock of precision machine tools, criminals will always be able to buy, steal, or make guns and ammunition.

As the experience of New York, Washington, D.C., and other cities with severe restrictions on guns demonstrates, banning guns disarms only the law-abiding, not the predators. When you disarm peaceful citizens, crime and violence explode.

Gun prohibition will foster a violent black market. Self-preservation is the most basic human drive. When Americans cannot buy guns and ammunition legally to protect themselves, they will buy them illegally.

America's experience with alcohol prohibition and the war on drugs shows us what to expect as guns are banned: lucrative and lawless black markets in guns and ammunition will develop, dominated by violent criminal gangs. Black-market gun profits will give organized crime enormous power. Thousands of people will be murdered in shootouts between rival gun gangs, with innocent victims often caught in the crossfire. Police, courts, and politicians will be corrupted by huge gun profits.

Black-market guns and ammunition will become more lethal. (No one is going to risk going to jail to buy a .22 or a pellet gun; besides, you will need a machine gun to protect yourself from the gun gangs.) There will be many accidental deaths from defective guns and ammunition manufactured in underground workshops.

The enormous violence and destruction created by gun prohibition will lead to public outcries that the government "do something." The government will respond with warrantless searches of cars, schools, office buildings, and homes for guns. Trial by jury will be severely restricted for most gun offenses. Hundreds of new prisons will be built to house millions of Americans arrested for possession of guns and trafficking.

Gun prohibition will increase police assaults and murders of innocent Americans. Gun prohibition will ultimately require gun confiscation and a war on guns, which will surely be even more bloody than the war on drugs. The violence we have witnessed between police and drug dealers is nothing compared to the violence you will see when police try to confiscate people's guns.

The gun confiscations have already begun. According to the *Washington Times*, "The 3rd Police District [has] adopted a policy of observing and questioning anyone who even gives the appearance of carrying a weapon." CNN News reports that in Boston, police publicly strip-search "suspicious" teenagers, searching for drugs and guns. The Police Foundation has called for random use of metal detectors on the streets to identify anyone who might be carrying a gun. Van-mounted magnetometers and other scanners are being developed to search homes and buildings.

In Chicago, Housing Authority Chairman Vincent Lane has organized door-to-door searches of public-housing apartments, without warrants, looking for drugs and guns. In Waco, Texas, "suspected firearms violations" was the justification the FBI and Bureau of Alcohol, Tobacco and Firearms used to attack the compound of the Branch Davidians—with machine guns, poisonous CS gas, and tanks. At least eighty-six men, women, and children were either shot to death, suffocated, or burned alive.

As gun prohibition intensifies, we can expect many more such attacks. In Washington, D.C., Mayor Sharon Pratt Kelley requested that President Clinton call out the National Guard to patrol the streets. Ross Perot told Texas Rangers that police should cordon off entire inner-city communities and conduct door-to-door searches for illegal drugs and firearms. In a speech in California, President Clinton endorsed police "sweeps" for illegal drugs and guns.

The war on drugs has established the legal precedents for expanding such paramilitary attacks. Dr. Arnold Trebach, founder of the Drug Policy Foundation, describes this scene of military occupation by the DEA in Northern California under the Campaign Against Marijuana Planting (CAMP):

> The residents of [Trinity County] were considered so hostile to law enforcement that Mr. Ruzzamenti [of the DEA] had said it was necessary "to virtually occupy the area with a small army"

for several days each year while eradication activities took place.

Residents were stunned and frightened to suddenly see strange men in combat uniforms, carrying military weapons, simply take over the entire area. "Many of these troops pointed their rifles at us, and one man was waving a .45 pistol at us when they went by. They were shouting 'War on drugs!' 'War on drugs!' and they took our pictures and some said they would be back." (Arnold Trebach, *The Great Drug War*, pp. 198–99.)

The image of paramilitary SWAT teams invading our homes and confiscating our guns is abhorrent to everything America stands for. Yet, that is precisely where gun prohibition is leading us.

Many of America's sixty-five million gun owners are not going to meekly surrender their guns. Millions consider gun ownership their inalienable right, and they will fight to preserve it.

The bitter irony of gun prohibition is that laws intended to reduce violence could spark the bloodiest violence in our history. We must stop gun prohibition now, before it is too late.

This essay originally appeared in the July and August 1994 issues of Freedom Daily, *published by The Future of Freedom Foundation.*

*B*efore a standing army can rule, the people must be disarmed; as they are in almost every kingdom in Europe. The supreme power in America cannot enforce unjust laws by the sword; because the whole body of the people are armed, and constitute a force superior to any band of regular troops that can be, on any pretense, raised in the United States.

—Noah Webster

3

The Assault-Weapons Scam

by James Bovard

The 1994 federal assault-weapons ban could be the first step towards legislation leading to the confiscation of tens of millions of private rifles, shotguns, and pistols. Though the bill Clinton signed purportedly targets only "assault weapons," the loose definitions and expansive goals of the antigun lobby will almost certainly lead to a vast expansion of weapons to be seized. And, as the experience of several states and New York City shows, the destruction of the Second Amendment via political demagoguery has already progressed much further than most Americans realize.

In recent years, four states and numerous cities and counties have banned or severely restricted the ownership of assault weapons. According to the Defense Department, an assault weapon is a rifle that is capable of both automatic (machine gun) fire and semiautomatic (one shot per trigger pull) fire. But most of the media implicitly defines "assault weapon" as any "politically incorrect rifle." Most bans focus on semiautomatic rifles, and media coverage routinely confuses semiautomatic with automatic machine guns, ownership of which has been severely restricted by the federal government since 1934. A study by David Kopel's Independence Institute of Denver noted:

> American civilians have owned semiautomatics since the 1890s, and currently an estimated twenty to thirty million own the firearms covered by the broader definitions of "assault weapon."

As a result of muddled definitions of assault weapons, bans on such guns have been extremely arbitrary. California in 1989 banned the sale or transfer of assault weapons and required all existing owners to register their guns. The California law was very poorly drafted—California Attorney General Dan Lungren later admitted that some of the gun models specifically banned by the California legislature did not exist. San Francisco lawyer Don Kates suggested that legislators, in compiling the list of prohibited guns, appeared to have selected from "some picture book . . . of mislabeled firearms they thought looked evil." The *Los Angeles Times* noted:

> Asked what action a police officer should take in dealing with an apparently illegal but misidentified gun, Lungren's press secretary, Dave Puglia, said local authorities "are going to have to use their discretion."

Thus, since the state legislature made a mess of the statute, local officials should have the arbitrary power to pick and choose which guns to ban and which gun owners to arrest and imprison.

The vast majority of Californians did not register their guns; thus, the law may have created as many as 300,000 new criminals. In numerous cases, police carrying out searches of people's homes have seized weapons they allege to be illegal assault weapons—and then refused to return them even after receiving proof that the guns are not legally banned under California law. The assault-weapons ban was enacted after politicians claimed that such guns were a grave public menace. But Torrey Johnson of the California Bureau of Forensic Services concluded in a confidential report:

> It is obvious to those of us in the state crime lab system that the presumption that [assault weapons] constitute a major threat in California is absolutely wrong.

In 1989, the Denver city council banned Denver residents from owning or selling so-called assault weapons. (Residents could apply for police permission to continue possessing weapons obtained prior to the date of the ban.) Denver even banned residents from using assault weapons for self-defense in their own homes—as if government officials were seeking to prevent citizens from having an unfair advantage against burglars or rapists who break into their homes. In February 1993, a local court struck down the law as unconstitutionally vague and a violation of the state constitution.

New Jersey in 1990 banned ownership of so-called assault rifles. Gov. Jim Florio declaimed: "There are some weapons that are just so dangerous that society has a right and the obligation even to take those weapons out of circulation." President Clinton considers the New Jersey law a model for the nation, declaring last October, "We need a national law to do what New Jersey has done here with assault weapons." But the ban was so extensive that even some models of BB guns were outlawed. Owners of the restricted guns were required to surrender them to the police, sell them to a licensed dealer, or render the guns inoperable. Yet, Ira Marlowe of the Coalition for New Jersey Sportsmen reported that "there was not one murder . . . with a semiautomatic assault weapon" in New Jersey in 1989, the year before the ban took effect. Joseph Constance, deputy chief of the Trenton, New Jersey, Police Department, told the Senate Judiciary Committee in August 1993:

> Since police started keeping statistics, we now know that assault weapons are/were used in an underwhelming .026 of 1 percent of crimes in New Jersey. This means that my officers are more likely to confront an escaped tiger from the local zoo than to confront an assault rifle in the hands of a drug-crazed killer on the streets.

New Jersey had an estimated 300,000 owners of "assault weapons," each potentially facing up to five years in prison for violating the state law.

New York City required rifle owners to register their guns in 1967; city council members at that time promised that the registration lists would not be used for a general confiscation of law-abiding citizens' weapons. Roughly one million New Yorkers were obliged to register with police. The *New York Times* editorialized on September 26, 1967:

> No sportsman should object to a city law that makes it mandatory to obtain a license from the Police Department and to register rifles. . . . Carefully drawn local legislation would protect the constitutional rights of owners and buyers. The purpose of registration would be not to prohibit but to control dangerous weapons.

In 1991, New York City Mayor David Dinkins railroaded a bill through the city council banning possession of many semiautomatic rifles, claiming that they were actually assault weapons. Scores of thousands of residents who had registered in 1967 and scrupulously obeyed the law were stripped of their right to own their guns.

Police are now using the registration lists to crack down on gun owners; police have sent out threatening letters, and policemen have gone door-to-door demanding that people surrender their guns, according to Stephen Halbrook, a lawyer and author of two books on gun control.

Halbrook notes that the New York ban "prohibits so many guns that they don't even know how many are prohibited" and that the law is so vague that the city police "arbitrarily apply it to almost any gun owner." Jerold Levine, counsel to the New York Rifle Association, observed: "Tens of thousands of New York veterans who kept their rifles from World War II or the Korean War have been turned into felons as a result of this law. Even the puny target-shooting guns in Coney Island arcades have been banned under the new law because their magazines hold more than five rounds." The motto of New York gun owners fighting the proposal was: "We Complied, They Lied." Jerry Preiser, president of the Federation of New York State Rifle and Pistol Clubs, declared that the mayor's and city council's acts "only show that New York City's leaders are like repeat sex offenders . . . they can never be trusted!"

The bans on assault weapons are products of political hysteria rather than a public safety campaign. A 1990 Florida state commission estimated that "only one-tenth of one percent of the guns used in crimes were so-called 'assault weapons.'" The FBI Uniform Crime Reports indicated that rifles of all kinds account for only 4 percent of the nation's homicides, and the number of homicides committed with rifles has fallen sharply in the last decade. William Poole, an Arizona public policy expert, observed, "This whole issue of identifying so-called 'bad firearms' is the intellectual equivalent of counting beer cans along the road and banning the most popular brands."

The federal law bans guns that have grenade-launcher and bayonet-mount attachments. But neither the U.S. Justice Department nor the Bureau of Alcohol, Tobacco and Firearms could provide a single example of either grenade launchers or bayonets attached to assault weapons being used in any violent crime in the United States. (Grenade launchers were used by the FBI in their final assault in Waco, but the FBI would not be affected by the bill.)

The federal assault-weapons ban is widely perceived as a foot in the door to far more extensive gun bans. When a *Christian Science Monitor* reporter asked Democratic Sen. Dianne Feinstein of California, the lead sponsor of the bill, why her amendment did not ban all semiautomatic guns, Feinstein replied: "We couldn't have gotten it through Congress." Democratic Rep. Charles Schumer of New York, declared, "We'll be carrying the Feinstein banner in the House when it comes to semiautomatic weapons."

If all semiautomatic guns were banned, the federal government would confiscate up to thirty-five million weapons. The Clinton administration has tentatively embraced a proposal to require all gun owners to be licensed—which could be a prelude to the type of gun confiscations ongoing in New York City.

Some of the rationales offered for banning assault weapons were almost comical. Senator Feinstein declared that assault weapons should be banned because they can fire many rounds "within seconds and without warning." Perhaps Senator Feinstein thinks that guns should be equipped with an official warning notice, such as a tape recording, announcing before firing: "Warning: Redneck May Pull Trigger in Five Seconds." Complaining that guns fire "without warning" makes as much sense as complaining that politicians talk before thinking.

The 1994 attack on assault weapons often showed the emotional fervor of an old-time gospel revival show. (President Clinton told a Washington church audience last August that it was "the will of God" that Congress approve his crime bill.) Yet, as with most holy wars, some of the warriors are not without the taint of hypocrisy. Sen. John Rockefeller, a West Virginia Democrat, was a fervent supporter of the crime bill and the assault-weapons ban. A few days after the bill had passed the Senate, the Charleston (West Virginia) *Daily Mail* reported from Washington:

> If burglars are casing big houses around here, they may want to give wide berth to the Rockefeller mansion. The occupant is packing heat and knows how to use it. Senator Jay Rockefeller disclosed that for the past 25 years, he has been the proud owner of a Colt AR-15, a so-called assault weapon used in Vietnam. Rockefeller keeps the rifle in his Washington home.

This was news to the police in Washington, D.C., where the ownership of AR-15s is banned. After Rockefeller was told that having such a gun in the District was a crime, he "remembered" that he actually kept the gun stored in northern Virginia. Rockefeller also claimed that he was unaware that the District of Columbia banned such guns. Rockefeller has private security guards around his lavish Washington home, and the Senate office buildings where he works are heavily guarded by well-fed Capitol policemen. Yet he still feels entitled to own a gun that he wanted to severely restrict other Americans from being able to purchase.

The assault-weapons ban, as it now stands, is based largely on blind faith in the BATF to administer a badly written law. The BATF has already indicated that, aside from the 19 guns named in the act, more than 160 other guns would be covered under the generic definitions offered in the bill. Given the vagueness of the law, vast numbers of Americans would likely unknowingly, unintentionally violate the law.

A June 1994 Supreme Court decision sheds invaluable light on how the assault-weapons ban will likely be administered. Harold Staples of Oklahoma owned a semiautomatic rifle—an AR-15; the BATF raided his home, found the gun, and confiscated it, claiming that it was actually a machine gun, i.e., an automatic weapon. (The National Firearms Act of 1934 bans possession of unregistered, unlicensed machine guns.)

The BATF argued in court that the gun had been illegally modified so that it could fire more than one bullet with each trigger pull—the technical definition of an automatic weapon. Staples swore that when he operated the gun, it fired only one shot per trigger pull, and functioned poorly at that. Each violation of the National Firearms Act can be punished by up to ten years in prison. (Stephen Halbrook notes that the BATF, after it confiscates a person's guns, sometimes tampers with the guns to make them shoot automatically—and then drags the person into court on trumped-up charges.)

The Clinton administration asserted that gun owners must be presumed guilty even in cases where they had no intention to break the law. The Supreme Court, in a 7–2 decision, rejected the administration's arguments; writing for the majority, Justice Clarence Thomas declared: "The government's position, is precisely that 'guns in general' are dangerous items. [For] the Government . . . the proposition that a defendant's knowledge that the item he possessed 'was a gun' is sufficient for a conviction." Justice Thomas pilloried the Clinton administration's position: "In the Government's view, any person . . . who simply has inherited a gun from a relative and left it untouched in an attic or basement, can be subject to imprisonment, despite absolute ignorance of the gun's firing capabilities, if the gun turns out to be an automatic."

The Clinton administration implicitly argued before the Supreme Court that gun owners are the legal equivalent of drug dealers. To justify their claim that gun owners must be presumed guilty, government prosecutors cited cases involving the presumption of guilt under the federal Narcotics Act of 1914. (At one point in the case, federal prosecutors argued that "one would hardly be surprised to learn that owning a gun is not an innocent act.") Since drug dealers are automatically assumed to know they are violating federal narcotics laws, the Clinton administration claimed that gun owners must be presumed to know when they violate federal gun laws. Yet the Constitution does not expressly guarantee citizens' right to sell crack, but it does expressly protect citizens' right to bear arms.

On the surface, the Staples decision was a major victory for gun owners. But federal bureaucrats and congressmen have rarely let court decisions long impede their efforts to further restrict Americans' liberties. The Staples decision raised hackles among supporters of the assault-weapons ban; Congressman Schumer told the *New York Times* that the bill may need to be amended to include a proof of intent to violate the law.

Yet, the final bill included no such requirement for proof of criminal intent. Thus, millions of Americans could face five-year prison sentences for such "crimes" as merely buying or possessing a rifle or pistol magazine that would hold more than ten bullets. (The act, in a leap of liberal creativity, defines gun magazines as assault weapons, even though a magazine by itself is harmless.)

The Clinton administration explicitly came out in favor of a ban on all semiautomatics last year. The Clinton administration's official federal budget presentation for 1995 (released in early 1994) announced: "The administration also supports a ban on semi-automatic firearms." Clinton administration officials later disavowed the statement, claiming that they didn't know how that sentence managed to get into the official budget plans of the president—as if the sentence was simply a typo caused by a malfunctioning spell-check program.

Assault-weapons laws resemble hate-speech laws. Hate-speech laws usually begin by targeting a few words of which almost no one approves. Once the system for controlling and punishing "hate speech" is put into place, there is little or nothing to stop it from expanding to punish more and more types of everyday speech. Similarly, once an assault-weapons law is on the books, there is little to prevent politicians from vastly increasing the number of weapons banned under the law.

Gun laws are an attempt to nationalize—to confiscate—the right of self-defense. Politicians perennially react to the police's total failure to control crime by trying to disarm law-abiding citizens. In a nutshell, gun control means that because criminals abuse guns, law-abiding citizens have no right to defend themselves. The worse government fails to control crime, the less right each individual

21

citizen has to defend himself. The guiding principle of handgun banners appears to be: No matter how badly the government fails to protect a citizen, the citizen still has no right to protect himself.

The political creeping repeal of the right to self-defense is a huge decrease in the modern American's liberty because the government has completely failed to fill the void. The government has stripped millions of people of their right to own weapons—yet generally left them free to be robbed, raped, and murdered. Gun control is one of the best cases of governments enacting laws that "corner" private citizens—forcing the citizen either to put himself into danger or to be a lawbreaker.

The 1992 Los Angeles riot illustrated why people cannot rely on police to protect their lives or their livelihoods. When mobs began looting, burning, and savagely assaulting defenseless individuals, the Los Angeles police turned tail and ran, leaving hundreds of business owners to see their life savings plundered.

When asked on the first day of the riot about the lack of police protection for people being beaten by mobs, Los Angeles Police Chief Daryl Gates replied: "There are going to be situations where people are going to go without assistance. That's just the facts of life. There are not enough of us to be everywhere." Gates later admitted that "a little panic and paralysis settled in" among police officers. Armand Arabian, a California Supreme Court justice, noted that if the Los Angeles Police Department had responded any slower to the riots, "we would have seen photos of policemen pasted on milk containers and listed as missing." While the police effectively ran away from the violent rioters, they did return later to seize the guns and handcuff some of the owners of Korean stores who fought to defend their property. The city government even banned law-abiding citizens from buying bullets or picking up previously purchased weapons after the riot began.

Economist Morgan Reynolds noted:

> The looters and arsonists tended to leave houses and apartment buildings in the riot areas of Los Angeles alone—not out of compassion, but because, as a 13-year old neighborhood resident said, "The residents got guns and everybody knows that. Nobody's going to mess with folks in houses."

The main effect of banning assault weapons is to give government an excuse to arrest or imprison millions of Americans while doing little or nothing to reduce crime. Regardless of what Congress intends in its assault-weapons ban, federal bureaucrats will stretch, twist, and contort the law to maximize their power over American citizens. For this reason alone, Congress should repeal the ban.

This essay originally appeared in the March and April 1996 issues of Freedom Daily, *published by The Future of Freedom Foundation.*

*N*o free men shall be debarred the use of arms.

—Thomas Jefferson

4

Gun Control, Patriotism, and Civil Disobedience

by Jacob G. Hornberger

The State of California recently enacted a law which requires owners of semiautomatic weapons to register their guns with the state. But when the law went into effect, thousands of California gun owners, although risking a felony conviction, refused to comply with its requirements.

The gun owners were immediately showered with harsh criticism, not only from their public officials but from many of their fellow citizens as well. The critics implied, among other things, that since the law had been passed by the duly elected representatives of the people, the gun owners, as members of society, had a duty to comply with its terms.

The controversy raises important issues concerning liberty, property, government, patriotism, and civil disobedience.

By adopting the welfare-state, planned-economy way of life in the twentieth century, the American people of our time have rejected and abandoned the principles of individual freedom and limited government on which our nation was founded. But they have also rejected and abandoned something of equal importance: the concept of patriotism that characterized America's Founding Fathers.

There have been two different notions of patriotism in American history. The one which characterizes the American people of the twentieth century—the one which is taught in our public schools—

is this: patriotism means the support of one's own government and the actions that the government takes on behalf of the citizenry. The idea is that since we live in a democratic society, the majority should have the political power to take any action it desires. And although those in the minority may not like the laws, they are duty-bound, as "good" citizens, to obey and support them.

The distinguishing characteristic of this type of patriotism is that the citizen does not make an independent, personal judgment of the rightness or wrongness of a law. Instead, he does what he has been taught to do since the first grade in his government-approved schools: he places unwavering faith and trust in the judgment of his popularly elected public officials.

The other concept of patriotism was the type that characterized the British colonists during the late 1700s. These individuals believed that patriotism meant a devotion to certain principles of rightness and morality. They believed that the good citizen had the duty to make an independent judgment as to whether his own government's laws violated these principles. And so, unlike their counterparts in America today, these individuals refused to automatically accept the legitimacy of the actions of their public officials.

Let us examine how "real-world" applications of these two concepts of patriotism differ dramatically.

In the late 1700s, the British colonists were suffering under the same type of oppressive regulatory and tax system under which present-day Americans are suffering. What was the reaction of the colonists to this regulatory and tax tyranny? They deliberately chose to ignore and disobey their government's regulations and tax acts. Smuggling and tax evasion were the order of the day! And the more their government tried to enforce the restrictions, the more it met with disregard and disobedience from the citizenry.

Sometimes smugglers or tax evaders would be caught and brought to trial. The result? Despite conclusive evidence of guilt and the judges' instructions to convict, the defendants' fellow citizens on the juries regularly voted verdicts of acquittal.

And civil disobedience was not limited to economic regulations and taxation. There was also widespread resistance to conscription, especially during the French and Indian War. Those who were conscripted deserted the army in large numbers. And those who had not been conscripted hid the deserters in their homes.

This was what it once meant to be a patriot—the devotion to a certain set of principles regarding rightness, morality, individualism, liberty, and property; and it meant a firm stand against one's own government when it violated those principles.

26

If an American of today were magically transported back to colonial America of the late 1700s, he would immediately find himself at odds with the colonists who were resisting the tyranny of their government. How do we know this? By the way in which Americans of today respond to what is a much more oppressive and tyrannical economic system: with either meekness or, even worse, ardent, "flag-waving" support for the actions of their rulers.

And what is their attitude toward their fellow citizens who are caught violating the rules and regulations? Again, either meekness or fervent support of their rulers. After all, what was the reaction to the Internal Revenue Service's seizure of Willie Nelson's property? "I'll make a small donation but otherwise don't get me involved—I don't want them coming after me!" And to the conviction of Michael Milken for violating such ridiculous economic regulations that even King George would have been embarrassed? "He got what's coming to him—he shouldn't have made so much money anyway!" And to Leona Helmsley's conviction for having taken improper deductions on her income tax return? "She's obnoxious—she should go to jail." The thought of rising to the defense of these victims of political tyranny is anathema to the present-day American "patriot."

And what about jury trials involving economic crimes? Like the good little citizens they have been taught to be, especially in their public schools, American "patriots" dutifully comply with the judge's instructions to convict their fellow citizens of violating this regulatory and tax tyranny. Although they have the same power as their ancestors to disregard the judge's instructions and to acquit their fellow citizens, the thought of doing so is repugnant to present-day "patriots." They choose instead to do their "duty" and thereby become "patriotic" agents of their own government's tyranny.

Therefore, there is no doubt that the American of today would feel very uncomfortable if, all of a sudden, he found himself in the British colonies in 1776 in the midst of smugglers, tax evaders, draft resisters, and other patriots of that time.

This brings us back to the individuals in California who are refusing to register their guns.

As our American ancestors understood so well, the bedrock of a free society is private ownership of property. And there are few rights of private ownership more important than the unfettered right to own weapons.

Why is ownership of weapons so vitally important? Not for hunting. And not even to resist aggression by domestic criminals or foreign invaders. No, as history has repeatedly shown the vital importance of the fundamental right to own arms is to resist tyranny by one's own government, should such tyranny ever become unendurably evil and oppressive.

The lesson which Americans of today have forgotten or have never learned—the lesson which our ancestors tried so hard to teach us—is that the greatest threat to our lives, liberty, property, and security lies not with some foreign government, as our rulers so often tell us; instead, the greatest threat to the well-being of all of us lies with our own government!

Of course, there are those who suggest that democratically elected public officials would never do anything seriously harmful to the American people. But let's look at just a few twentieth-century examples. They confiscated people's gold. They repudiated gold clauses in government debts. They provoked the Japanese into attacking Pearl Harbor and then acted as though they were surprised. They incarcerated Japanese-Americans for no crime at all. They injected dangerous, mind-altering drugs into American servicemen without their knowledge. They radiated the American people in the Pacific Northwest and then deliberately hid it from them. They have surreptitiously confiscated and plundered people's income and savings through the Federal Reserve System. They have terrorized the citizenry through the IRS. And, most recently, they have sent our fellow citizens to their deaths thousands of miles away in the pursuit of a relatively insignificant cause.

Those who believe that democratically elected rulers lack the potential and inclination for destructive conduct against their citizenry are living in la-la land.

Of course, the proponents of political tyranny are usually well motivated. Those who enacted the gun-registration law in California point to those who have used semiautomatic weapons to commit horrible, murderous acts. But the illusion—the pipe-dream—is that bad acts can be prevented through the deprivation of liberty. They cannot be! Life is insecure—whether under liberty or enslavement. The only choice is between liberty and insecurity, on the one hand, and insecurity and enslavement on the other.

The true patriot scrutinizes the actions of his own government with unceasing vigilance. And when his government violates the morality and rightness associated with principles of individual freedom and private property, he immediately rises in opposition to his government. This is why the gun owners of California might ultimately go down in history as among the greatest and most courageous patriots of our time.

This essay originally appeared in the May 1991 issue of Freedom Daily, *published by The Future of Freedom Foundation.*

To preserve liberty, it is essential that the whole body of the people always possess arms, and be taught alike, especially when young, how to use them.

—Richard Henry Lee

5

Real Independence Day: The Meaning of the Second Amendment

by Richard J. Davis, D.D.S.

There is no national holiday on April 19 (or April 18), though the Boston Marathon is run around this time. When I was in college in the East, this meant not only mid spring but midterm, and when exams were finished, the anniversary of Paul Revere's ride seemed a perfect excuse for a party. Though I've celebrated this date habitually over the years, the party spirit has faded a bit with age, and I've begun to reflect a little more on those events and people of 1775. What went on in the minds of those small-town farmers that made them stand up and challenge the army of "their" government—coincidentally, the most powerful one on earth at that time? Were they pushed to it accidentally, or had they already drawn the line beyond which they would stand and fight?

It's a question that may relate to today more than we realize. Our government is, at least for now, undoubtedly the most powerful in the world. It holds power that those Massachusetts farmers couldn't have imagined. It intrudes in our lives to a degree that would have astonished and appalled them. Are we drawing a mental line of how far we'll let it go? Are we waiting until somebody unintentionally pushes us too far? Are we past standing up for our rights altogether? It's hard to tell.

There are several movements, both within and without the government, aimed at disarming the American population. The argument seems to be that we are so civilized that we have no good use for such things as firearms. In 1775, the goal of the British troops marching on Concord was similar—to disarm the colonists. They weren't after individual personal weapons; they were after cannon and large stores of gunpowder rumored to be at Concord. (With the limited technology of the day, cannon were the largest technological advantage the British had over the colonists.)

The government today has numerous large technological advantages over the civilian population. There remain a substantial number of heavily regulated, registered weapons in private hands, but the closest thing to technological parity is the common semiautomatic weapon available to the general public. It is this class, mislabeled "assault weapons," that currently comes under the most vigorous attack from gun control advocates both inside and outside government. The usual attack centers around the "fact" that they have "no sporting uses."

Ignoring the inaccuracy of this "fact," the truth is that the Second Amendment makes no reference to "sporting uses." In fact, it seems most unlikely that "sporting uses" were a consideration for those who framed the Bill of Rights. Unfortunately, even the National Rifle Association skirts timidly around the real issue, as if it were too much for Americans to deal with. The point of the Second Amendment is to give American citizens the capability to assemble rapidly as an armed militia for their own collective defense. This has generally been thought of as defense against an invading foreign enemy, but recent events in Los Angeles and Waco clearly point out that other situations might also create such a need. To the Framers of the Bill of Rights, the most recent "foreign enemy" was the perceived tyranny of their own government—in England, but, nonetheless, at that time (1775), their own. A great concern of the writers of the Bill of Rights was that the government they were then forming might eventually become tyrannical, and that the citizens needed protection from that possibility—hence the entire Bill of Rights, including the Second Amendment.

There are past examples of armed citizen resistance to the perceived tyranny of the U.S. government: the Whiskey Rebellion, Shays's Rebellion, and most notably the War Between the States. The fact that none of these was successful does nothing to alter the principle of armed resistance as a last resort. The fact that a large number of citizens exercise their Second Amendment rights unquestionably admits the possibility of future armed resistance and can properly be a sobering thought for those in government. The amount of support for gun control within the government (those sworn to uphold and defend the Constitution, *including* the Bill of Rights, *including* the Second Amendment) perhaps indicates that this is indeed the case. As the existence of our nuclear missiles served as a brake to Soviet ambitions for forty-five years, so a well-armed populace must serve as a brake on those in government who might abuse their authority.

The removal of firearms from civilian hands removes this restraint from government. However small the actual possibility of revolt, whatever the theories that we are "too civilized" to need or want firearms, the fact remains that the ultimate guarantor of political power, here as anywhere else in the world, is the possession of (and willingness and ability to use if necessary) firearms. Without that, not only is resistance to unjust laws or abuse of power impossible, but enforcement of *just* laws is impossible.

Does this mean that we need to plan for armed resistance? Hardly. The odds are far less, even than in 1860. Only massive public support for resistance would give it a chance of success, and such support could well prevent the need for resistance through political means. Only a blatant usurpation of power in excess of authority might try to override such resistance, and the coup attempt in Russia illustrates that massive resistance can succeed even with little or no violence.

Maybe we *do* need to give more thought to where we draw the line. How much power do we really grant to the federal government? If the power is accumulated gradually enough, it may not be blatant enough to inspire massive resistance. In that case, a smaller group might be suddenly and accidentally pushed beyond its limit and provide the tragedy of a Lexington-like spark, with violent, armed resistance the final result. In either case, without the Second Amendment, we lose much of our option to resist. Even the most massive nonviolent resistance becomes fatally or near-fatally weak without the threat of *armed* resistance to back it. Two old quotes come to mind: "The price of liberty is eternal vigilance" and "Those who give up essential liberty to purchase a little temporary safety deserve neither liberty nor safety." It's time we paid a little more attention to where we stand before it's too late.

Here on the Eastern Shore, guns are a way of life. People like to hunt, people like to shoot, and people like to collect guns out of historical or aesthetic interest. Most small towns could easily arm an infantry company out of private collections, and small cities could probably arm a regiment—possibly including automatic or other heavy weapons. There are no militia groups, but organization could occur around fire companies, fraternal organizations, gun clubs, and even veterans' organizations if the provocation were severe enough.

I doubt I will ever have to stand and literally fight for my rights. I hope I don't. If it's going to happen, I hope it happens after my lifetime, after my children's lifetimes, and, if and when they arrive, after my grandchildren's lifetimes. I suspect that's about as many generations ahead as we're capable of worrying about.

At the same time, I wonder whether that isn't what those Massachusetts farmers felt in 1775. No doubt, resistance to the British Army looked as hopeless to them as resistance to the federal government does to me. But if it does come to lining up on the village green, I hope I'll have the courage to stand with my neighbors—and they the courage to stand with me—to make sure America stays a free country of free people.

We celebrate that freedom on the Fourth of July, but those words of July Fourth were created by the actions of those men in April 1775. In my mind, that's the real holiday, in the original sense of the word.

This essay originally appeared in the January 1994 issue of Chronicles *(Volume 18, No. 1), published by The Rockford Institute, 934 N. Main St., Rockford, IL 61103. It was reprinted by permission in the June 1994 issue of* Freedom Daily, *published by The Future of Freedom Foundation.*

6

What the Second Amendment Means

by Sheldon Richman

T he decline of education in the United States may be reflected in the high correlation between the amount of formal schooling a person has and his inability to understand the following words: "A well regulated Militia, being necessary to the security of a free State, the right of the people to keep and bear Arms, shall not be infringed."

The radio and television talk shows have been raging in recent years with discussions of the Second Amendment to the U.S. Constitution. The debate is whether that amendment protects private, individual ownership of firearms or means something else. Typically, people who favor gun ownership take the first position, although some legal scholars who do not like gun ownership reluctantly agree that the amendment protects it nonetheless. Opponents of guns argue that the amendment protects only the right of the states to form militias or National Guard units. As the American Civil Liberties Union of Southern California has put it, "The original intent of the Second Amendment was to protect the right of states to maintain militias." Dennis Henigan of Handgun Control, Inc., says the amendment is "about the distribution of military power in a society between the federal government and the state. That's all they [the Framers] were talking about." As he put it elsewhere, "The Second Amendment guaranteed the right of the people to be armed *as part of* a 'well regulated' militia, ensuring that the arming of the state militia not depend on the whim of the central government." (Emphasis added.)

Thus, we have diametrically opposed individualist and collectivist interpretations of the amendment. People on both sides of the issue agree, however, that the sentence was not well written. I disagree. A knowledge of English syntax and vocabulary—and nothing else—should be sufficient to determine that the amendment protects an individualist right to firearms.

Approaching the sentence as grammarians, we immediately note two things: the simple subject is "right" and the full predicate is "shall not be infringed." This, in other words, is a sentence about a right that is already assumed to exist. It does not say, "The people shall have a right to keep and bear arms." The amendment *recognizes*, but does not grant, the right. As the U.S. Supreme Court wrote in the late nineteenth century, the right to keep and bear arms is independent of the Constitution.

That has important implications for the opening militia phrase, which confuses so many people. Gun opponents often argue that if the opening phrase does not apply—if, say, the standing army takes the place of the militia—then the right to keep and bear arms is nullified. That view would require a willingness by the Framers of the Constitution to agree to this statement: If a well-regulated militia is not necessary to the security of a free state, the right of the people to keep and bear arms shall (or may) be infringed. But it is absurd to think that the Framers would embrace that statement. Their political philosophy would not permit them to speak of a permissible infringement of rights. In their view, individuals, joining together to form a political unit, delegate rights and powers to government. But the people do not—cannot—consent to an *infringement* of their rights; such consent, logically, would make no sense. The term *infringement* implies lack of consent.

As a matter of logic, it is an error to believe that nullification of the opening phrase would nullify the main clause. Imagine a long-lost constitution that stated: "The earth being flat, the right of the people to abstain from ocean travel shall not be infringed." Would anyone seriously argue that discovery of the earth's spherical shape would justify compelling people to sail?

The advocates of gun control maintain that the amendment merely affirms the states' right to form state militias. You want to own a gun? they ask. Join the National Guard. That view dissolves under even casual analysis. First, James Madison's amendment says "the right of the people." If he meant states, why didn't he say so? The Bill of Rights, in fact, never ascribes rights to states. On the other hand, the people are mentioned in the First, Fourth, Ninth, and Tenth Amendments, as well as in the Second. Surely the Framers did not mean to say that states have a right to peaceably assemble and be secure in their persons, houses, papers, and effects. The states are mentioned in the Tenth Amendment, but in terms of powers, not rights. Moreover, that amendment names both the people and the states, indicating that the Framers wrote "states" when they meant states and "people" when they meant people.

The meaning that the gun controllers impose on the amendment simply cannot be squared with the Framers' syntax and choice of words. If their concern had been to keep the national government from limiting the states' power to form militias, they might have written: "A well regulated militia being necessary for the security of a free state, the power of the States to form and control militias shall not be limited." (That, however, would have conflicted with other clauses in Article I of the Constitution.) The main clause of my revision keeps the focus on states and militias, where the gun controllers say it should be. In contrast, Madison's main clause focuses on the people's right to keep and bear arms. How can it be reasonably concluded that the amendment means anything but that the people have an unconditional right to own and carry arms?

To see this more clearly, consider that Madison's original draft reversed the order of the elements: "The right of the people to keep and bear arms shall not be infringed; a well armed and well regulated militia being the best security of a free country." That sentence implies that the way to achieve the well-armed and well-regulated militia necessary to the security of a free state is to recognize the right of people to own guns. In other words, without individual freedom to own and carry firearms, there can be no militia. ("Well regulated," Alexander Hamilton wrote in the *Federalist Papers*, meant well drilled and disciplined.)

How do we know that the "well regulated militia" is defined in terms of an armed populace and not vice versa? The syntax of the sentence tells us. Madison and his colleagues in the House of Representatives chose to put the militia reference into a dependent phrase. They picked the weakest possible construction by using the participle "being" instead of writing, say, "Since a well regulated militia is necessary. . . ." Their syntax keeps the militia idea from stealing the thunder of what is to come later in the sentence. Moreover, the weak form indicates that the need for a militia was offered not as a reason (or condition) for prohibiting infringement of the stated right, but rather as the reason for enumerating the right in the Bill of Rights. (It could have been left implicit in the Ninth Amendment, which affirms unenumerated rights.)

The House reversed the elements of Madison's amendment. That changed the emphasis, but not the meaning. In fact, the reversal made it a better sentence for the Bill of Rights. As adopted, the amendment begins by quickly putting on the record the most important reason for its inclusion in the Bill of Rights but without dwelling on the matter; that's what the weak participle, "being," accomplishes. The sentence then moves on to the main event: "the right of the people to keep and bear arms." The Framers correctly intuited that in a Bill of Rights, the last thing the reader should have ringing in his mind's ear is the absolute prohibition on infringement of the natural right to own guns.

The lack of conflict between the militia and individual ownership of guns is made all the more clear by the fact that in the Framers' day, the militia comprised, as George Mason put it, "the whole people." Thus, the amendment, rather than being muddled or contradictory, is elegant and appropriate to its task.

Finally, even if we grant the gun controllers' arguments about the Second Amendment, they still would not get where they want to go. In their view, the amendment authorizes the creation of state militias. But that implies no prohibition on private gun ownership. And the Ninth Amendment says, "The enumeration in the Constitution of certain rights shall not be construed to deny or disparage others retained by the people." So the people have unenumerated rights. By what warrant can we exclude from those rights the right to keep and bear arms?

This essay originally appeared in the October 1995 issue of Freedom Daily, *published by The Future of Freedom Foundation.*

7

The Right to Life Equals the Right to Possess Firearms

by Sheldon Richman

In the opinion of the pundits, the tide has turned on the gun control issue. After years of successful opposition to federal gun control by the National Rifle Association and others, the public is said to be ready for limits on gun ownership. The most recent evidence is passage of the federal Brady Bill, requiring a five-day waiting period for the purchase of handguns, during which the would-be buyer's background could be checked by police. Proponents of the waiting period readily concede that it will not curb crime; rather, they see it as a first step toward further control of handguns and rifles, misleadingly called "assault weapons." President Clinton has said he wants federal registration and licensing of gun ownership and a ban on such semiautomatic weapons.

The gun control issue is so overgrown with brush that essentials get obscured. Rather than exchanging endless statistical studies about what did or did not happen when this or that state liberalized or tightened its gun laws, we need to look afresh at the roots of this important matter and see what has too long been overlooked: gun control strikes at every individual's right to life, liberty, and the pursuit of happiness.

In spelling out why this is so, I wish to acknowledge a debt to Jeffrey R. Snyder, an attorney in Washington, D.C., for making that elementary point in a landmark article, "A Nation of Cowards," in the Fall 1993 issue of *Public Interest*. Sometimes overlooking the obvious is the simplest thing in the world. When someone shows you what is right under your nose, that person deserves praise. Jeffrey Snyder is in that position.

If you own your life, then you have the right to defend yourself against anyone who would deprive you of it. I can't imagine anyone's taking issue with that statement. And if you have the right of self-defense, it follows that you have the right to act (in ways, of course, that violate no other rights) to obtain means appropriate to that defense. That brings us to firearms, particularly the handgun, which so many people would outlaw. The handgun has been called the equalizer ("God made men, but Sam Colt made them equal"), and for good reason. It affords smaller, weaker people the chance to defend themselves against bigger, stronger people who threaten them. Handguns offer the otherwise defenseless a convenient, practical, inexpensive method of safeguarding themselves and their families. Banishing handguns—even if the big and the strong were also denied them—would leave the small and the weak defenseless. The big and the strong aggressors have other tools of violence at their disposal; the small and the weak do not have other effective means of self-defense.

Thus, outlawing handguns is a denial of the right of self-defense and, perforce, the right to life. It is absurd to claim to uphold those rights while denying the right to own handguns. But that is not all. Any restriction on handgun ownership—including outlawing the carrying of handguns—represents the same violation of the right to life. That includes waiting periods, registration, right-to-carry licenses, and the rest.

But, many people will say, in a civilized society, we have delegated our right of self-defense to the government. We don't need to carry guns. Here is the crux. We cannot delegate our right of self-defense. I am not talking about morality now. In the most practical sense, it is impossible to delegate our right to self-defense or, for that matter, our responsibility to defend our families. Why? Not even the most idealized vision of government has ever promised to protect each individual twenty-four hours a day. The most it promises is a general deterrence through police patrols and apprehension of criminals. (Leave aside the fact that the government's record of delivering on its promises is abysmal.) Simply put, the government leaves us unprotected nearly all the time. In fact, government law-enforcement personnel have no legal obligation to protect you even if they see a crime in progress.

The upshot is that anyone who believes he has turned his self-defense over to government is living in a dream world. Self-defense remains the right and responsibility of the individual. That is an unalterable fact of life. There is no choice in the matter.

Since government cannot—and makes no attempt to—protect citizens at all times, even so-called moderate gun control interferes with the right of self-defense. Take the waiting period. Can the state guarantee that an applicant for a handgun will not be victimized during the five-day wait? Of course not. The state thus forces applicants to be vulnerable to aggression while it decides whether they are worthy of an indispensable method of self-defense. What about registration and licensing? The licensing power, of course, entails the possibility of an applicant's being turned down for a license. Furthermore, registration and licensing have been used countless times in the past to carry out a wholesale confiscation of guns. The Clinton proposal, therefore, would put all peaceful people at risk of having their means of self-defense taken away.

Other regulations similarly put innocent people in harm's way. Virginia's law limiting gun purchases to one per month interferes with the self-defense rights of someone who wishes to buy guns for home and workplace. Laws against carrying a handgun leave people vulnerable when they are on the street. It is no accident that most crime occurs outside of people's homes. Criminals know that one in two homes has a gun, but very few people are permitted to carry a gun. Thus, they know it is safer to attack someone who is away from his home. (In England, where gun ownership is more severely restricted, more crime occurs in people's homes. According to David Kopel, in Britain 59 percent of attempted burglaries occur in occupied homes; in the United States, it's 13 percent. "Fear of being shot convinces most American burglars to strike empty targets," he writes in *The Samurai, the Mountie, and the Cowboy*.)

But there are already too many guns in society, the proponents of control say. More guns would make society more violent. Would it? The issue is not a matter of numbers. What counts is not how many guns, but who has them. Today, the people who would use guns to violate rights have little trouble getting them, while those who would use them to defend their rights have increasing trouble getting them. That is an undeniable truth that refutes the gun controllers who say they want to reduce violent crime. Someone who intends to rob people is not likely to respect gun laws. Most guns used in crimes were not bought by the criminal at a gun store. They were bought on the black market or stolen. The bottom line is that gun control, regardless of the proponents' intentions, harasses rights defenders and barely touches rights violators. Gun control is, in effect, a subsidy for criminals.

To be sure, gun accidents happen, and were there no guns, there would be no gun accidents. But the number of gun accidents has been falling for years and represents a minuscule percentage of the some sixty-six million handguns Americans possess. Meanwhile, according to researcher Gary Kleck, Americans use handguns (without necessarily firing) in self-defense 645,000 times each year, and surveys of convicted criminals show an understandable desire to avoid armed victims.

A much-touted study purporting to show that a handgun in the home greatly increases the odds that an innocent person will be killed ignored all the cases in which merely brandishing the gun succeeded in protecting innocent people. Terrible incidents—such as the mass murder at Luby's Cafeteria in Killeen, Texas, and on the Long Island Railroad—would be less likely if people were free to carry handguns. Even if such an incident occurred, fewer people might be killed, because one of the armed bystanders would wound or kill the assailant. That happens at least as frequently as the shooting of a group of unarmed victims, but it rarely is reported in the national news media. (Shortly after the Luby's incident, an armed citizen saved twenty Shoney's restaurant customers from armed robbers in Anniston, Alabama.) The possibility of accident and the probability that some will use guns to kill themselves (which, after all, violates no one's rights) are not good reasons to interfere with the right of self-defense.

The gun controllers think they can shut up their opponents by conjuring images of the Wild West. But as much research shows, the frontier was not nearly as violent as the movies would have us believe. It stands to reason: if most people are armed both with guns and the knowledge of how to use them, violent crime is deterred. In our time, we have seen just those results in Florida and Oregon after those states liberalized their license-to-carry laws.

"An armed society," wrote libertarian science-fiction writer Robert Heinlein, "is a polite society." An armed people is a people who have taken a personal interest in keeping their society civil. David Kopel reports that 81 percent of the "good Samaritans" who help victims of violent crime are gun owners. The state has failed to protect us—we should never have expected it to. The time is now for us to take control of our own destiny.

This essay originally appeared in the June 1994 issue of Freedom Daily, *published by The Future of Freedom Foundation.*

The great object is that every man be armed. . . . Everyone who is able may have a gun. . . . Are we at last brought to such a humiliating and debasing degradation that we cannot be trusted with arms for our own defense?

—Patrick Henry

8

Gun Control:
A Historical Perspective

by Benedict D. LaRosa

Gun control is an issue that never stands on its own. By this I mean that the motives behind it are rarely those expressed by its advocates. There is almost always a hidden agenda.

On rare occasions, those proposing the confiscation of weapons are candid about their motives. Such was the case in Japan in 1588 when the Shogun Hideyoshi disarmed the populace during what came to be called the Great Sword Hunt. He decreed: "The possession of unnecessary implements [of war] makes difficult the collection of taxes and dues, and tends to foment uprisings."

The motivation behind gun control is much the same today; it's just that our politicians are not as candid as Hideyoshi.

The Japanese populace has been disarmed ever since.

The Anglo-American tradition is much different. But before I discuss our own heritage, I'd like to tell you a little-known but tragic story of a people who disarmed for the sake of peace.

The story is that of the Roman destruction of Carthage in 146 B.C. At the time, Carthage, though defeated and forced to pay tribute to Rome, was not completely disarmed and was still a prosperous city-state. Too prosperous, in fact, for Rome.

Cato, who presided over the Roman Senate, ended every speech, no matter what the subject, with the words: "Besides, I think that Carthage must be destroyed."

The pretext came when Carthage attempted to defend itself against raids by the Numidians. By treaty, Carthage could not make war without Rome's consent. The Romans were deaf to pleas from Carthaginian envoys.

When Carthage declared war on Numidia in 151 B.C., Rome in turn declared war on Carthage. Carthage attempted to negotiate her way out of this dilemma. Rome promised to preserve the freedom and integrity of Carthage in exchange for 300 children of the noblest families as hostages, and a promise to obey whatever order the consuls gave. The Carthaginians reluctantly agreed.

Despite this assurance, Rome secretly sent an army and fleet to Utica, a neighbor of Carthage, and then demanded the surrender of all weapons, ships, and a huge amount of grain. When these conditions had been met, and the people and nation of Carthage had been disarmed, the Romans next demanded the populace move ten miles from the city so that they could then burn it to the ground without hindrance.

The Carthaginan ambassadors argued in vain before the Roman consuls at the betrayal. They had exchanged the means to defend themselves for a promise from their most likely oppressors. Without striking a blow, the Romans had reduced a mighty nation against which they were unable to compete commercially to a defenseless mass of humanity.

When the people of Carthage realized what had happened, they went mad. They dragged their leaders through the streets, stoned them, and tore them limb from limb. They killed without hesitation those who had advised surrendering their arms. Some wept in the empty arsenals.

With a resolution they should have shown when the crisis began, the Carthaginians reformed their army and attempted to rearm themselves. They demolished public buildings and melted down statues to make the implements of war. In two months of frenzied work, they produced 8,000 shields, 18,000 swords, 30,000 spears, 60,000 catapult missiles and 120 ships!

Carthage resisted the Roman siege for three years. In the end, her preparations were too little, too late. She could not make up for the damage done in surrendering her means to resist years earlier. Once the walls of the city had been scaled, the fighting was street by street without quarter, and the snipers so intense that the Roman commander, Scipio Aemilianus, ordered captured streets to be set on fire and leveled, thereby killing thousands of Carthaginians hiding in the ruins. The slaughter lasted six days.

The city's population had been reduced from 500,000 to 55,000 during its siege and capture. The survivors were sold as slaves, the city pillaged and then burned to the ground, its soil plowed and sown with salt. All Carthage's dependencies who had stood by her were destroyed. The city burned for seventeen days.

The Romans wanted to teach the world a lesson. They did. Our Anglo-Saxon forefathers learned it well, which is why we still have the tradition of a well-armed citizenry mistrustful of government as a potential oppressor or betrayer.

Armed individuals organized into voluntary home-defense units called militias are not unique to the Anglo-Saxon tradition. Assyria depended on such militias as long ago as 1,000 B.C.

The backbone of the early Greek and Roman armies consisted of highly patriotic, sturdy peasants organized into citizen militias.

In fourth-century India, men in various trades and crafts armed themselves and trained as soldiers. Although kings hired and levied these guild militias, they were treated with suspicion because they tended to usurp the ruler's power.

The Byzantine Empire of the Middle Ages depended heavily upon the guerrilla tactics of home-guard units to assist in repelling invaders.

In Europe, it was local militias that first confronted the Viking raiders. And it was the English militiamen at the Battle of Hastings who initially broke William the Conqueror's left wing, though the battle was eventually lost.

In eleventh-century China, the expense of maintaining a large standing army against constant threats of invasion drove the emperor to rely instead on conscript militias for border and local security. This allowed him to reduce his standing army by half while increasing the men under arms seven times.

It is, however, the thirteenth-century English longbowmen, many of whom were yeomen militia, to whom we trace the modern concept of a well-regulated militia. At a time when the rest of Europe was moving from feudal levies to mercenary forces, England and, a little later, France relied heavily upon yeomen militias.

During the fifteenth century, the French used militia forces to neutralize marauding bands of mercenaries between wars.

It was masses of popular militias that saved Muscovy in 1612 from Polish and Swedish invaders.

Militia forces were used throughout Europe during the Middle Ages as primary defense forces, to complement regular or mercenary troops, and in law-and-order roles. In fact, the rank of private comes from the sixteenth century, when individuals who provided their own arms and equipment contracted to serve as private soldiers among feudal levies.

The early British colonists, imbued with the English distrust for standing military establishments as a threat to civil liberties, incorporated the tradition of the citizen-soldier. In 1636, the first militia unit, the North Regiment of Boston, was formed, followed two years later by the Ancient and Honorable Artillery Company, the oldest American military unit in existence.

One of the first acts of Parliament following the accession of William and Mary to the throne of England as a result of the Glorious Revolution of 1688 was to restore the old constitution with its provision that every man may arm for self-defense.

In 1760, Britain began adopting mercantilist policies toward her American colonies. By 1768, they had produced such hardships and a reversal of the previous prosperity that British troops had to be sent to suppress riots and collect taxes.

Between 1768 and 1777, the British policy was to disarm the American colonists by whatever means possible, from entrapment, false promises of safekeeping, banning imports, and seizure to eventually shooting persons bearing arms.

By 1774, the British had embargoed shipments of arms to America, and the Americans responded by arming themselves and forming independent militia companies.

On the night of April 18, 1775, General Gage, governor of Massachusetts, dispatched several hundred soldiers of the Boston garrison under the command of Major Pitcairn to seize the arms and munitions stored by the illegal colonial militias in Concord.

When Pitcairn encountered the Minutemen on the Lexington common blocking his way, he demanded that they throw down their arms and disperse. Although willing to disperse, the Minutemen were not willing to surrender their arms. The rest is history.

Three days after the British retreat from Concord, General Gage refused to allow Bostonians to leave the city without depositing their arms and ammunition with a selectman at Faneuil Hall, to be returned at a suitable time after their return. When the citizens of Boston foolishly complied, Gage seized the arms and refused to permit their owners to leave the city. ("Declaration of the Causes and Necessity of Taking up Arms," July 6, 1775.)

The news of Gage's seizure of the arms of Bostonians not engaged in hostilities and rumors of British troops sailing from England to seize the arms of the colonists swept the colonies.

The colonists considered these actions a violation of their constitutionally guaranteed right to have and use arms for self-preservation and defense, as indeed they were.

In 1777, William Knox, undersecretary of state for colonial affairs, advocated for the American colonies the creation of a ruling aristocracy loyal to the Crown, the establishment of the Church of England, and an unlimited power to tax. To prevent resistance to these measures, Knox proposed disarming all the people:

> The Militia Laws should be repealed and none suffered to be reenacted & the Arms of all the People should be taken away, & every piece of Ordnance removed into the King's Stores, nor should any Foundry or manufacture of Arms, Gunpowder, or Warlike Stores, be ever suffered in America, nor should any Gunpowder, Lead, Arms, or Ordnance be imported into it without License; they will have but little need of such things for the future, as the King's Troops, Ships, & Forts will be sufficient to protect them from danger.

We hear the same argument today. You don't need arms for your own protection. The police and military will protect you. The question is, who will protect us from the protectors?

Let's look at a few recent examples in history of armed and disarmed populaces.

A shining example of the former is Switzerland. Like America, Switzerland won its independence in a war fought by armed citizenry. Since independence in the fourteenth century, the Swiss have been required to keep and bear arms, and since 1515, have had a policy of armed neutrality. Its form of government is similar to the one set up by our Founders—a weak central government exercising few, defined powers having to do mostly with external affairs and limited authority over internal matters at the canton (state) and local levels.

The Swiss boast that they have the weakest central government in the West. They feel a strong central government weakens citizen initiative and individual responsibility. I wonder where they got that idea!

A Swiss publication states, "The Swiss do not have an army, they are the army." The eighteenth-century economist Adam Smith considered Switzerland the only place where the whole body of the people were successfully drilled in militia skills. As far back as 1513, Machiavelli commented in his book *The Prince*, "The Swiss are well armed and enjoy great freedom."

Gun ownership is a matter of community duty, for the Swiss consider national defense too important to be left to professional soldiers or those who join the army to learn civilian job skills.

Every able-bodied male from about age 21 receives seventeen weeks of military training, and for the next thirty years engages in decreasing increments of mandatory training amounting to about one year of direct military service. He then serves on reserve status until age 50 or 55. Enlisted men take home automatic assault rifles and officers their pistols, ammunition, and necessary equipment and supplies. Voluntary marksmanship training is common. Almost anyone can purchase surplus machine guns, antiaircraft and anti-tank weapons, howitzers, and artillery pieces, as Americans could at one time. Yet the crime rate is so low, statistics aren't even kept.

In 1978, the Swiss refused to ratify a Council of Europe Convention on Control of Firearms. Switzerland was then pressured by other European governments to adopt a law barring foreigners from purchasing guns in Switzerland that they could not purchase in their own countries and requiring a license for Swiss citizens. Outraged citizens forced the central government to abandon any idea of such a law, and the one canton that had enacted similar legislation had it overturned the following year in a referendum.

A popular story at the turn of the century concerned an earlier visit by the crown prince and later kaiser of Germany, Wilhelm Hohenzollern, to view the Swiss militia in training. He supposedly asked the Swiss commander how many men he had under arms. When the commander answered one million, Wilhelm asked what would happen if five million of his men crossed the Swiss border tomorrow. The Swiss commander replied that each of his men would fire five shots and go home.

No one knows whether this had anything to do with the scrapping of the German plan to flank France at the onset of World War I by passing through the northern Swiss lowlands, or of the French plan to attack the German flank through Switzerland, but most Swiss and many historians think it did.

During World War II, Hitler coveted the Swiss gold reserves and needed lines of supply and communications through Switzerland to supply Axis forces in the Mediterranean. An analysis of Switzerland's well-armed citizenry, mountainous terrain, fortifications, and civil-defense preparations persuaded German military planners to forgo an invasion.

The Afghans are a recent example of an armed populace who, though backward and using mostly outdated weapons, drove the Soviet invaders from the country and overthrew a puppet government. You can bet the Afghans don't believe in gun control.

The U.S. army troops who perpetrated the Wounded Knee massacre in 1890 first persuaded their intended victims to disarm. The villagers at My Lai were unarmed. Throughout history, the greatest atrocities have been inflicted upon the unarmed.

In 1920, the British government disarmed its populace on the pretext of reducing crime. The real reason was the ruling class's fear of a popular revolution, for the bankruptcy of the British nation which had occurred in 1916 and the staggering casualties suffered in the war had been kept from the British people. By 1919, in the face of massive unemployment and starvation, and expected loved ones' not returning, the truth could no longer be hidden.

In retrospect, the fear of a violent revolution was exaggerated. But the crime rate has done nothing but increase since the gun grab.

Since ancient times, well-armed individuals organized into militia units were not only the best method of preventing one noble or chief from gaining too much power but also the least costly way of using limited manpower to defend the community or tribe.

In today's technological society, it is still true that well-armed and trained individuals, especially when organized into locally led militia units, are a threat to centralized control.

When a nation's policy is defensive, militias are generally adequate and successful, as in the case of Switzerland. But our forefathers knew that every nation that disarmed its citizens, and that ceased to depend upon militias for its defense, relying instead upon standing armies, inevitably embarked upon an imperialistic policy abroad and authoritarian rule at home and eventually destroyed itself.

Machiavelli understood this lesson of history, for he wrote in the early sixteenth century that it is a "legally armed" citizenry which had kept governments "free and incorrupt. . . . Rome remained free for four hundred years and Sparta eight hundred although their citizens were well armed at the time; but many other states that have been disarmed have lost their liberties in less than forty years."

Our Constitution is eloquent testimony to the distrust of our forefathers for government and its monopoly on force. Article I, Section 8 of that document authorizes Congress "to raise and support

51

Armies," limiting appropriations to two years. Yet, the very next clause authorizes Congress "to provide and maintain a Navy," without restrictions on appropriations. Giving authority to raise and support in one case with funding limitations but providing and maintaining in the other without funding limitations shows their distrust for standing armies, navies by themselves not being a threat to liberty. Further in that article, Congress is given authority not to raise and maintain a militia, but to call it forth "to execute the Laws of the Union, suppress Insurrections and repel Invasions" as well as to organize, arm, and discipline it. The federal government has authority only to govern that part of the militia that "may be employed in the Service of the United States," leaving to the States the authority to appoint its officers and train its members.

We should take alarm at the 20,000-odd laws across this country restricting the right to keep and bear arms and the recent attempts by public officials and private organizations to further encroach upon this right, for as George Mason observed, over two hundred years ago, "To disarm the people . . . [is] the best and most effectual way to enslave them."

Or as Noah Webster, his contemporary, remarked, "Before a standing army can rule, the people must be disarmed."

Richard Henry Lee, who first proposed independence at the Continental Congress of 1776, warned, "To preserve liberty, it is essential that the whole body of the people always possess arms, and be taught alike, especially when young, how to use them."

To which we may add the comments of Elbridge Gerry, a signer of the Declaration of Independence: "Whenever governments mean to invade the rights and liberties of the people, they always attempt to destroy the militia, in order to raise an army upon their ruins."

Since ancient times, weapon control and game laws have been used by ruling elites to dominate populations, prevent effective resistance to their arbitrary rule, and to maintain a subservient labor force. Only those with a license were allowed to hunt, these eventually being restricted to the gentry and those in political favor. Even Blackstone in his *Commentaries* remarked, "Prevention of popular insurrections and resistance to the government by disarming the bulk of the people . . . is a reason oftener meant, than avowed, by the makers of the forest and game laws." By mere coincidence, only licensed hunting is legal today even on private property, and hunters are under increasing attack. Could the motivation be the same?

Let's face it, the only reason for gun registration is eventual gun confiscation. And the only reason behind gun confiscation is eventual tyranny.

Josh Sugarmann, former communications director of the National Coalition to Ban Handguns, wrote recently in the *Washington Monthly*: "Handgun controls do little to stop criminals from obtaining handguns." Then why the recent hysterical campaign for gun control? Sugarmann answers this question by stating that he and his associates favor gun control not to disarm criminals, but because they believe Americans cannot be trusted with guns.

The question remains, trusted to do what?

Just as with the British ruling elite following World War I, they have kept from the American people the knowledge of the catastrophic effects of their political and economic policies which are coming home to roost, and of the impending authoritarian measures they intend to implement to maintain their rule. They rightfully deduce that enough of us will realize who is at fault as the scarcity of food and work become more acute and crime more plentiful, and will no longer fall for their divide-and-conquer tactic of shifting the blame for our woes to foreigners making better goods, to illegal aliens taking away our jobs, to drug pushers threatening our national security, and will instead hold them accountable.

This is why the campaign to disarm Americans is so spontaneous, coordinated, and unrelenting. They know that our other rights are unenforceable without the means to secure them. And that Americans who have sought and continue to seek every peaceful means of redressing grievances are about to run out of patience in the face of economic collapse, social upheaval, and increasingly venal and arbitrary legislation and law enforcement.

Just as the British policy banning the importation of arms and ammunition in 1774 alerted our forefathers to the government's true motives and led them to form militias throughout the colonies, so President Bush's ban on the importation of certain firearms in March 1989 and other gun control measures have awakened quite a few patriotic Americans and moved them to join our political ranks.

Ultimately, it was the possession and expert use of firearms that made American independence attainable. Patrick Henry admonished future generations to "guard with jealous attention the public liberty. Suspect everyone who approaches that jewel. Unfortunately, nothing will preserve it but downright force. Whenever you give up that force, you are ruined."

Only time will tell whether enough Americans have learned the lessons of history or whether we will suffer the consequences of apathy and unpreparedness.

This essay is based on a speech Benedict D. LaRosa gave at the Texas Libertarian Party Convention in San Antonio, Texas, on June 9, 1990. Reprinted by permission. For a reprint of this essay in pamphlet form, send $2.00 to Benedict D. LaRosa, 13423 Blanco Road, #181, San Antonio, TX 78216. This essay was reprinted in the June and July 1994 issues of Freedom Daily, *published by The Future of Freedom Foundation.*

9

The Nazi Mind-Set in America

by Jacob G. Hornberger

Before the end of World War II, in 1944, Friedrich A. Hayek, who was later to win the Nobel Memorial Prize in Economic Science, startled the Western world with a book entitled *The Road to Serfdom*. Hayek argued that despite the war against Nazi Germany, the economic philosophy of the Nazis and communists was becoming the guiding light for American and British policymakers. In a later forward to the book, Hayek wrote:

> But after war broke out I felt that this widespread misunderstanding of the political systems of our enemies, and soon also of our new ally, Russia, constituted a serious danger which had to be met by a more systematic effort. Also, it was already fairly obvious that England herself was likely to experiment after the war with the same kind of policies which I was convinced had contributed so much to destroy liberty elsewhere. . . .
>
> Opinion moves fast in the United States, and even now it is difficult to remember how comparatively a short time it was before *The Road to Serfdom* appeared that the most extreme kind of economic planning had been seriously advocated and the model of Russia held up for imitation by men who were soon to play an important role in public affairs. . . . Be it enough to mention that in 1934 the newly established National Planning

Board devoted a good deal of attention to the example of planning provided by these four countries: Germany, Italy, Russia, and Japan.

As the fiftieth anniversary of the end of World War II approaches, Americans must ask themselves a troubling question: Did Hayek's concerns become reality—have Americans, in fact, traveled the road to serfdom the past fifty years? Or, to put it another way, did the Nazis lose the military battles but win the war for the hearts and minds of the American people?

Consider, for example, the Nazi economic system. Who can argue that the American people do not believe in and support most of its tenets? For example, how many Americans today do not unequivocally support the following planks of the Nationalist (Nazi) Party of Germany, adopted in Munich on February 24, 1920:

> "We ask that the government undertake the obligation above all of providing citizens with adequate opportunity for employment and earning a living."
>
> "The activities of the individual must not be allowed to clash with the interests of the community, but must take place within its confines and be for the good of all. Therefore, we demand: . . . *an end to the power of the financial interests.*"
>
> "We demand profit sharing in big business."
>
> "We demand a broad extension of care for the aged."
>
> "We demand . . . the greatest possible consideration of small business in the purchases of the national, state, and municipal governments."
>
> "In order to make possible to every capable and industrious [citizen] the attainment of higher education and thus the achievement of a post of leadership, the government must provide an all-around enlargement of our entire system of public education. . . . We demand the education at government expense of gifted children of poor parents. . . ."
>
> "The government must undertake the improvement of public health—by protecting mother and child, by prohibiting child labor . . . by the greatest possible support for all clubs concerned with the physical education of youth."
>
> "[We] combat the . . . materialistic spirit within and without us, and are convinced that a permanent recovery of our people can only proceed from within on the foundation of *The Common Good Before the Individual Good.*"

I repeat: How many Americans today do not unequivocally support most, if not all, of these Nazi economic and political principles?

And if there is any doubt whether the Nazi economic philosophy did, in fact, win the hearts and minds of the American people, consider the following description of the Nazi economic system by Leonard Peikoff in his book *The Ominous Parallels*:

> Contrary to the Marxists, the Nazis did not advocate public ownership of the means of production. They did demand that the government oversee and run the nation's economy. The issue of legal ownership, they explained, is secondary; what counts is the issue of *control*. Private citizens, therefore, may continue to hold titles to property—so long as the state reserves to itself the unqualified right to regulate the use of their property.

What American objects to these principles of the Nazi economic system? Don't most Americans favor the planned economy, the regulated economy, the controlled economy? Don't most Americans favor the type of economic controls, and the right of government to institute such controls, that characterized the Nazi society: wage and price controls, high taxes, government-business partnerships, licensing, permits, and a myriad other economic regulations?

The truth is that Hayek's warning was ignored. Having defeated the Nazis in battle, Americans became ardent supporters and advocates of Nazi economic policies.

Why? Part of the answer lies in another feature that was central to the Nazi way of life: public schooling. "Oh, no! You have gone too far this time," the average American will exclaim. "Public schooling is a distinctively American institution—as American as apple pie and free enterprise." The truth? As Sheldon Richman documents so well in his book, *Separating School & State*, twentieth-century Americans adopted the idea of a state schooling system in the latter part of the nineteenth century from—you guessed it—Prussia! And as Mr. Richman points out, public schooling has proven as successful in the United States as it did in Germany. Why? Because it has succeeded in its goal of producing a nation of "good little citizens"—people who pay their taxes on time, follow the rules, obey orders, condemn and turn in the rule-breakers, and see themselves as essential cogs in the national wheel. Consider the words of Richard Ebeling, in his introduction to *Separating School & State*:

In the hands of the state, compulsory public education becomes a tool for political control and manipulation—a prime instrument for the thought police of the society. And precisely because every child passes through the same indoctrination process—learning the same "official history," the same "civic virtues," the same lessons of obedience and loyalty to the state—it becomes extremely difficult for the independent soul to free himself from the straightjacket of the ideology and values the political authorities wish to imprint upon the population under its jurisdiction. For the communists, it was the class struggle and obedience to the Party and Comrade Stalin; for the fascists, it was worship of the nation-state and obedience to the Duce; for the Nazis, it was race purity and obedience to the Führer. The content has varied, but the form has remained the same. Through the institution of compulsory state education, the child is to be molded like wax into the shape desired by the state and its educational elite.

We should not believe that because ours is a freer, more democratic society, the same imprinting procedure has not occurred even here, in America. Every generation of school-age children has imprinted upon it a politically correct ideology concerning America's past and the sanctity of the role of the state in society. Practically every child in the public school system learns that the "robber barons" of the 19th century exploited the common working man; that unregulated capitalism needed to be harnessed by enlightened government regulation beginning in the Progressive era at the turn of the century; that wild Wall Street speculation was a primary cause of the Great Depression; that only Franklin Roosevelt's New Deal saved America from catastrophe; and that American intervention in foreign wars has been necessary and inevitable, with the United States government required to be a global leader and an occasional world policeman.

This brings us to the heart of the problem—the core of the Nazi mind-set: that the interests of the individual must be subordinated to the interests of the nation. This is the principle that controls the minds of the American people, just as it controlled the minds of the German people sixty years ago. Each person is viewed as a bee in a hive; his primary role in life is to serve the hive and the ruler of the hive, and to be sacrificed when the hive and its ruler consider it necessary. This is why Americans of our time, unlike their ancestors, favor such things as income taxation, Social Security, socialized medicine, and drug laws; they believe, as did Germans in the 1930s, that their bodies, lives, income, and property, in the final analysis, are subordinate to the interests of the nation.

As you read the following words of Adolf Hitler, ask yourself which American politician, which American bureaucrat, which American schoolteacher, which American citizen would disagree with the principles to which Hitler subscribed:

> It is thus necessary that the individual should finally come to realize that his own ego is of no importance in comparison with the existence of his nation; that the position of the individual ego is conditioned solely by the interests of the nation as a whole; that pride and conceitedness, the feeling that the individual . . . is superior, so far from being merely laughable, involve great dangers for the existence of the community that is a nation; that above all the unity of a nation's spirit and will are worth far more than the freedom of the spirit and will of an individual; and that the higher interests involved in the life of the whole must here set the limits and lay down the duties of the interests of the individual.

Even though the average American enthusiastically supports the Nazi economic philosophy, he recoils at having his beliefs labeled as "Nazi." Why? Because, he argues, the Nazi government, unlike the U.S. government, killed six million people in concentration camps, and this mass murder of millions of people, rather than economic philosophy, captures the true essence of the Nazi label.

What Americans fail (or refuse) to recognize is that the concentration camps were simply the logical extension of the Nazi mind-set! It does not matter whether there were six million killed—or six hundred—or six—or even one. The evil—the terrible, black evil—is the belief that a government should have the power to sacrifice even one individual for the good of the nation. Once this basic philosophical premise and political power are conceded, innocent people, beginning with a few and inevitably ending in multitudes, will be killed, because "the good of the nation" always ends up requiring it.

Political killings of innocent people could never happen in America, our fellow citizens tell us. America is a democracy. But so was Nazi Germany. Hitler was popularly elected, and his economic policies were widely favored and acclaimed (by Germans *and* Americans!).

But there is another basic problem with that assertion: it is happening here in America. And like the German people of the 1930s, Americans either refuse to see it happening, or they rationalize what is happening so that they do not have to deal with it. Now it is true that the killings do not number in the millions—but they certainly do number, so far, in the thousands.

Let's take some examples. The Branch Davidians at Waco, Texas: U.S. Army tanks and gas were used against peaceful, religious, well-armed people. More than eighty Americans, including children, were gassed and burned. And is there any remorse—any regret—any independent governmental investigation into this massacre? Not on your life. The government officials, just like their Nazi counterparts, think they did "the right thing" in killing our fellow citizens. And for those of you who look to the judiciary for protection, you had better look elsewhere: the federal judge who presided over the trial of the Waco survivors declared that he would not permit the government to be "put on trial," and then slapped forty-year sentences on the Branch Davidian survivors.

Or take Randy Weaver, his wife, and son, of Idaho. First, they were set up on an idiotic gun charge. (Weaver sold a shotgun that was a quarter of an inch too short, at the request of a U.S. government agent.) Then, they sent Weaver a notice of a wrong trial date. When he failed to appear, they surrounded his house and attacked. A government sniper plugged his unarmed wife in the head with a bullet as she was holding her baby. And they shot Weaver's son in the back. Then, at Weaver's trial, they fabricated evidence and committed perjury. Fortunately, Weaver was acquitted. But have any criminal charges been brought against the government agents for the murder of Weaver's wife and son? Did the federal judge in the case even cite the agents for contempt for their reprehensible conduct? Well, did the Nazi government ever bring charges against the SS? Did Nazi judges ever punish Nazi officials for killing Jews?

Government officers killed Donald Scott, a millionaire rancher in California. They claimed that they needed to barge into his house in the middle of the night in order to look for marijuana. And when Scott obeyed their order to lay down the gun he had picked up in his fear of the intruders, they shot him dead. And it later turned out that they had hoped to find marijuana so that they could confiscate his land and convert it to a national park.

But Americans either look the other way, the way the Germans did, or they rationalize what is happening by saying, "The war on drugs has gotta be won."

And it is not just killings. Just as the Nazis did, they are confiscating people's money, land, boats, cars—anything they can get their hands on. No longer do they need to depend only on taxes for their revenues—they just go grab the money and property directly and keep it, regardless of the guilt or innocence of the victims. And, of course, it's all rationalized because "the war on drugs has gotta be won."

And it's not just confiscations. It is also terror—the terror of Internal Revenue Service agents barging into people's homes, "visiting" them at work, and levying liens on bank accounts and real estate without any notice, hearing, or other semblance of due process.

Yes, it's true—we are not dealing with the killings and mass confiscations and infliction of terror on millions of people. It is happening only to several thousands. But that's today. What happens in a crisis? Suppose an American ruler decides he is not going to get "pushed around" by the ruler of North Korea, Haiti, Panama, Iraq, or Japan? What happens if a war is not over in a few weeks, but instead drags out into months, even years, with higher taxes, more controls, and . . . conscription? What happens if Americans, who are already being taxed 50 percent of their incomes, now find taxes at 60 or 70 percent? What happens if there is a massive tax strike in which millions refuse to pay their taxes? What happens if hundreds of thousands of American students refuse to be drafted by a president who refused to be drafted?

Will the government meekly surrender? Will it simply agree to lose "international face"? Not on your life. The Internal Revenue Service, the Department of Justice, the FBI, and the army will simply turn their massive powers against the leaders of the tax revolt and as many of its followers as possible. And they will do whatever is necessary to teach those "draft-dodging cowards" a lesson. The American people will learn what the German people learned: that the omnipotent state that loves the poor and the needy will remove its velvet glove and use its iron fist to smash those who interfere with the "good of the nation."

Let's look at some more examples of the Nazi mind-set in America—this time in the Department of the Army. The army conducted nuclear radiation experiments on American soldiers. Why? Because the good of the nation required it. The army conducted drug experiments on American citizens. Why? Because the good of the nation required it. The army conducted disease experiments on the American people. Why? Because the good of the nation required it. The army herded innocent Americans of Japanese descent into American concentration camps. Why? Because the good of the nation required it. The army entered into joint ventures with German Nazis at the end of World War II. Why? Because the good of the nation required it.

In other words, in the past, U.S. government officials have engaged in evil, Nazi-like conduct for the "good of the nation." Would they do so again? You can bet your life they would, if the good of the nation required it, and even if it entailed the violation of every single restriction on governmental power set forth in the U.S. Constitution.

There is nothing inevitable in all of this. Through the power of ideas, we can reverse the trend. If ideas did not matter, governments would not try to suppress ideas. Ideas do matter; they do have consequences; they do influence people into acting, into changing, into reversing course.

But the rights guaranteed by the First Amendment—the right to speak, to write, to disseminate ideas—are not sufficient. The ultimate safeguard against the ultimate tyranny lies instead with the right to bear arms guaranteed by the Second Amendment. If this Amendment is destroyed or severely constricted, the rest of the Constitution becomes worthless, because in a crisis in which their power base is threatened, and in which there are no means of forcible resistance, government officials will squash the things they view as "technicalities"—free speech, habeas corpus, trial by jury, and the other rights guaranteed in the Constitution.

Combine a crisis with a disarmed, discontented citizenry, and the concentration camp for hundreds of thousands becomes a real possibility. But when the citizenry, together with various patriotic sheriffs, police, and members of the armed forces, have the means to inflict severe casualties on their potential oppressors, tyrants think twice before they try to oppress their own citizens too heavily.

That is why every single effort to restrict or control or manage the ownership of guns must be resisted. The ultimate barrier to the ultimate tyranny lies not with the ballot box. It lies not with the soapbox. It lies not with the jury box. The ultimate barrier to the tyranny of one's own government lies with the cartridge box.

Contrary to everything our rulers tell us, and everything that our schoolteachers are teaching the children of this nation, the biggest threat to the lives and well-being of the American people lies not with some foreign government. The biggest threat to the American people today lies with the United States government. And while gun ownership stands as a barrier to potential, Nazi-like behavior, the long-term solution is to dismantle, not reform, the iron fist of the welfare state and the controlled economy. This includes the end (not the reform) of the IRS, the DEA, the BATF, the SEC, the FDA, HUD, the departments of HHS, Labor, Agriculture, and Energy, and every other agency that takes money from some and gives it to others or interferes with peaceful behavior. It entails the repeal of all laws that permit such conduct. And it means the privatization of most of the bureaucrats who work for the U.S. government.

But it also entails the end of potential oppressors who, in the past, have shown no reluctance to engage in evil, malicious, illegal, Nazi-like conduct against American citizens, such as the CIA and the standing army.

Would this mean that the U.S. government would not be permitted to act as the international Roman emperor? That is exactly what it would mean. But what about threats of invasion of the United States? Such threats are virtually nonexistent. But if every single citizen is free to arm himself to the teeth, any nation contemplating invasion would know that attacking the United States would be like swallowing a porcupine. What about a quick mobilization? There would be no reason why citizen-soldiers would not quickly mobilize in the event of an emergency. For example, suppose that the standing army is disbanded. The members of the 82nd Airborne Division would not simply disappear. They would become private, productive citizens, but ready in times of peril to answer the call. They could be, and probably would be more than willing to be, at any location in the country within 24 hours.

Moreover, there would be a doubly positive effect in terms of economic prosperity. No longer would taxes have to be sucked out of the pockets of private citizens to support the armed forces. And the members of the armed forces, now privatized, would now be economically productive members of society.

In his book *The Road to Serfdom*, Friedrich Hayek warned Americans in 1944 that despite their military war against the Nazis, they were traveling the philosophical and economic road that the Nazis and the communists were traveling. Our grandparents and parents ignored Hayek's warning. Now, we are left with the consequences: a government of omnipotent size and power using its power to kill innocent, peaceful citizens and confiscate millions of dollars of property to feed its insatiable hunger for more power. Today, the number of victims is in the thousands. But at the end of this road lie the concentration camps for the multitudes.

Can the tide be reversed? Can the omnipotent state be dismantled, rather than simply reformed? Yes. It will take a return to first principles—the principles on which this nation, not Germany, were founded: principles that hold that it is the individual, not the collective, that is supreme; that each individual has been endowed by his Creator with unalienable rights; that among these rights are life, liberty, and the pursuit of happiness; that to secure these rights, governments are instituted among men, deriving their just powers from the consent of the governed; that whenever any government, including the American government, becomes destructive of these ends, it is the right of the people to alter or abolish it and to institute new government; and that no individual—his life, liberty, or property—shall ever be sacrificed for the good of the nation. As Ayn Rand put it thirty years ago in her essay, "The Fascist New Frontier":

> If you wish to oppose [statism], you must challenge its basic premises. You must begin by realizing that there is no such thing as "the public interest" except as the sum of the interests of individual men. And the basic, common interest of all men— all *rational* men—is freedom. *Freedom* is the first requirement of "the public interest"—not *what* men do when they are free, but *that* they are free. All their achievements rest on that foundation—and cannot exist without it.
>
> The principles of a free, non-coercive social system are the only form of "the public interest." Such principles did and do exist. Try to project such a system. In today's cultural atmosphere, it might appear to you like a journey into the unknown. But—like Columbus—what you will discover is America.

This essay originally appeared in the August and September 1994 issues of Freedom Daily, *published by The Future of Freedom Foundation.*

10

Citizen Exploitation Isn't New

by John L. Egolf Jr.

Recent news that the U.S. government subjected as many as 800 people to radiation as part of an experimental program during the Cold War era, and Energy Secretary Hazel R. O'Leary's acknowledgment and recommendation of compensation for the victims is cause for deep concern and is also a symptom of a far wider and deeper sickness infesting the U.S. government.

The details from the *Washington Post* are sickening to Americans who value the sentiments in the Declaration of Independence and the Constitution.

Radiation tests were conducted on thirty mentally retarded teenagers. These unfortunate victims were fed radiation-enriched cereal. Other victims of these tests were injected with plutonium, one of the most dangerous carcinogens known to medical science. What is also disturbing is that while many Americans reacted with horror and shock, they also reacted as if this recent disclosure were an isolated case of government misconduct.

The U.S. government has routinely subjected Americans to medical experiments. This has been done without the victims' knowledge or consent. The U.S. Department of Health and the Alabama State Health Department ran the infamous Tuskegee experiment. The experiment started around 1932 and didn't end until 1972.

A group of poor black Alabamians had a positive diagnosis for syphilis. The medical authorities, instead of treating the disease, let the disease run its course. The victims were carefully researched from detection to autopsy.

What started as a racially motivated experiment on black citizens in the United States ended up as a bureaucratic nightmare for the victims. Many doctors from various backgrounds in the United States were involved in the experiment. The contempt for these victims is well documented in the histories of the experiment. Governments at all levels are increasingly contemptuous of the sacred rights of each individual person.

Another more recent example of medical experimentation condoned by even the U.S. Supreme Court is described in the case *United States, et al. v. James B. Stanley.* In 1958, James B. Stanley was administered LSD by the army without his knowledge or consent. The drug induced personality changes that resulted in his discharge from the military and the dissolution of his marriage.

When Stanley discovered what the U.S. government did to him, he sued and the case was eventually brought to the Supreme Court. Believe it or not, the high court ruled in favor of the government in 1987. When government officials tell people to "say no to drugs," perhaps they should also say, "Leave that to us."

The events described in this article could be multiplied many times. They are symptoms of a far wider and deeper evil. It is common for U.S. government officials to treat the citizens as objects instead of individuals having inherent worth.

Too many Americans and government officials have never learned or have forgotten the sacredness of human life. These experiments are conducted on the same evil premises that motivated the terrible human experimentation conducted in Nazi Germany. Those who are advocating a national health system should reevaluate their ideas and wonder what safeguards, if any, are to be imposed to protect future victims from unwanted experimentation.

In conclusion, Americans must evaluate these evil experiments in the light of the Declaration of Independence. In that document, each individual is regarded as having "unalienable rights" in his person, liberty, and pursuits. Yet, the prevailing ideological sentiments in the United States are very much against individual rights.

These incidents of human experimentation should cause each of us deep concern. Americans need to soberly evaluate the ideas and sentiments that went into the founding of this nation.

This article originally appeared in the January 6, 1994, issue of The Monroeville Journal. *It was reprinted by permission in the August 1994 issue of* Freedom Daily, *published by The Future of Freedom Foundation.*

*B*esides the advantage of being armed, which the Americans possess over the people of almost every other nation, the existence of subordinate governments . . . forms a barrier against the enterprises of ambition. . . . [The] several kingdoms of Europe . . . are afraid to trust the people with arms.

—James Madison

11

Waco and the Cult of the Omnipotent State

by Jacob G. Hornberger

David Koresh and his followers challenged the cult of the omnipotent state. And for that, they paid the ultimate price—death at the hands of United States governmental officials. The message was a powerful one for American serfs: "As long as you behave and obey, everything will be fine; but dare to challenge us, and you will pay the price."

The cult of the omnipotent state has millions of followers in the United States. Americans of today view their government in the same way as Christians view their God: they worship and adore the state, and they render their lives and fortunes to it. Statists believe that their lives—their very being—are a privilege that the state has given to them. They believe that everything they do is—and should be—dependent on the consent of the government. Thus, statists support such devices as income taxation, licensing laws, regulations, passports, trade restrictions, and the like.

A branch of the statist cult is that of the Christian-statists. The followers of this cult acknowledge the existence of God by Sunday attendance in church. But they believe that Caesar—the state—should still reign supreme over their lives. An example of a Christian-statist prayer would be:

"O mighty state, we worship and adore you. You provide us our sustenance when we are in need—our food, our housing, our medical care, our schooling. Our other God says that it is only through the sweat of our brow that we shall eat bread. But He is in error. For you provide us our daily bread with no sweat at all. You make us good, O mighty state, because you provide welfare for the poor, the elderly, businessmen, foreigners, and all others who benefit from your largess. We praise you, O mighty state. We give you thanks."

Statists made much to do about the kookiness of the Branch Davidians, e.g., their belief that David Koresh was Jesus Christ. But their kookiness was nothing compared to the kookiness of believing that the state is a god who, through coercion, is able to make people good, caring, and prosperous.

Moreover, by focusing on the beliefs of the Branch Davidians, rather than on their own beliefs, Christian-statists ignore some very important points. First, by supporting the welfare state, Christian-statists have rendered unto Caesar their lives, their economic activities, and the fruits of their earnings. Second, by supporting the state's interference with people's peaceful choices through the regulated economy, they have denigrated the God-given gift of free will. And third, by supporting the taxation that takes from some to give to others, they have actively involved themselves in the violation of God's commandment against stealing.

David Koresh and his followers committed a heinous crime in the eyes of the statist cultists: they pledged ultimate allegiance to God rather than Caesar. While the Branch Davidians may not have had a sound understanding of the philosophical framework of the statist cult and all of its ramifications, one thing is clear: Koresh and his followers refused to idolize the state. They recognized what true Christians throughout history have recognized: that a government whose laws violate the laws of God is evil and, therefore, that it is the duty of Christians to follow the laws of God, even at the expense of their lives.

The Ownership of Arms

But the Christians at Mount Carmel committed another heinous crime in the eyes of the statists: they accumulated weapons to defend themselves from the evil conduct of U.S. governmental officials.

While the state permits the serfs to do such things as write letters to the editor, publish books, vote, and so forth, it will not permit them to engage in conduct that threatens the state's omnipotent control over the citizenry. And the accumulation of arms— especially high-powered ones—threatens that control.

Therefore, acquiring a few guns to shoot geese or burglars is permitted by the state. But accumulating massive amounts of arms to

70

defend one's self from the state is considered a major offense—and death without trial is the threatened punishment.

Actually, though, the right to own arms has very little to do with geese and burglars. The right to own arms has one primary purpose: to ensure that governmental officials do not become too tyrannical.

Since ancient times, rulers have disarmed the citizenry with the intent of taking control over their lives. Rulers have always understood that when the citizenry is disarmed, the state can more easily enforce its orders. The key to a meek and compliant people, as history has so clearly shown, is a disarmed citizenry.

Our American ancestors clearly understood this. They remembered that taxes and regulations had precipitated the Revolution, but they also recalled that there had been one immediate cause for the war: their own governmental officials had attempted to confiscate their arms!

When is the use of arms against governmental officials justified? When it is the only means by which people can defend themselves from the evil conduct of their own government. When the lawmaker and the law-enforcer become the lawbreakers, it is the right and duty of the citizenry to meet force with force.

When public officials use force to engage in evil conduct against the citizenry, some people choose not to resist the evil—they submit to the tyranny peacefully; or they turn away when others are subjected to the tyranny; or they support the tyranny, usually out of fear. Others resist the evil, either within their own minds or openly through speech or force; they fear God much more than they do death at the hands of the state.

Sin vs. Evil

In justifying their incineration of the Branch Davidians, U.S. governmental officials made much to do about the sinfulness and evil of David Koresh and his followers. But sinfulness and evil are not the same. In his book *People of the Lie*, the noted psychiatrist M. Scott Peck explained:

> Sin is nothing more and nothing less than a failure to be continually perfect. Because it is impossible for us to be continually perfect, we are all sinners. . . . Evil is defined as the exercise of political power—that is, the imposition of one's will upon others by overt or covert coercion—in order to avoid . . . spiritual growth. In other words, the evil attack others instead of facing their own failures. . . . Evil people feel themselves to be perfect. . . . Since the evil, deep down, feel themselves to be

faultless, it is inevitable that when they are in conflict with the world they will invariably perceive the conflict as the world's fault. Since they must deny their own badness, they must perceive others as bad. They *project* their own evil onto the world. They never think of themselves as evil; on the other hand, they consequently see much evil in others. . . . Strangely enough, evil people are often destructive because they are attempting to destroy evil. The problem is that they misplace the locus of the evil. Instead of destroying others they should be destroying the sickness within themselves.

Conclusion

Fifty years ago, in his book *The Road to Serfdom*, Friedrich Hayek argued that Americans were traveling the same road that all others in history, including the communists, fascists, and Nazis, had traveled. People scoffed. But Americans did indeed travel that road. Believing they could exchange the liberty bestowed by God for the siren-song of governmental security, Americans instituted their welfare state and their managed economy. And now they are discovering the horrible truth: by abandoning the principles of their ancestors, they have neither liberty nor security.

What is the solution for the American people? To abandon the cult of the omnipotent state—to dissociate themselves from, and openly oppose, the evil actions of their own government—to acknowledge that their support of the welfare state and the managed economy was not only an economic error but a sinful one as well—to stand for the repeal, not the reform, of this evil and immoral way of life—to recognize that their lives, liberties, and property are rights endowed in them by God, not privileges given by government—to move toward the ideas and ideals of America's Founding Fathers—*and to pledge never again to become serfs on the plantation.*

This essay originally appeared in the September 1993 issue of Freedom Daily, *published by The Future of Freedom Foundation.*

12

Terrorism—
Public and Private

by Jacob G. Hornberger

On April 19, 1995, the federal building in Oklahoma City was bombed. Hundreds of people, including children, were killed or injured. Although federal government officials have been sporadically killed in the line of duty in the past, this was the first mass killing of federal civil servants in American history.

There was tremendous shock, anger, and outrage over the Oklahoma City massacre. While most Americans, of course, did not personally know the victims, there was a deep sense of mourning for them and their friends and relatives. It was one of those events that could remain in our consciousness for the rest of our lives—like the day John F. Kennedy was killed. (See "JFK, the CIA, and Conspiracies" by Jacob G. Hornberger, *Freedom Daily*, September 1992.)

The government arrested Timothy James McVeigh and charged him with the bombing. If Mr. McVeigh did, in fact, commit the act, there are strong indications that his motivation was to exact revenge for the deaths of eighty Branch Davidians, including children, in Waco, Texas, two years ago. The government announced that it will seek the death penalty for Mr. McVeigh and any others who are accused of the bombing.

But even if all of the participants in the Oklahoma City bombing are executed, that is not going to solve the central problem in this country. The bombing is the manifestation of a deep cancer that pervades the United States. But it is not the cancer itself.

All of us feel the pain associated with private acts of terrorism. The problem, however, is this: Millions of Americans cannot bring themselves to recognize a deeply uncomfortable possibility—that their own government engages in murder and terrorism against its own citizens.

Fifty years ago, in 1944, Friedrich A. Hayek, who would later win the Nobel Memorial Prize in Economic Science, wrote a book entitled *The Road to Serfdom*. (A fiftieth-anniversary edition was recently published, with an introduction by Milton Friedman, another Nobel Prize-winning economist.) Hayek argued that although the United States (and Great Britain) was waging war against the Nazis, the United States had, in fact, adopted the statist and collectivist economic programs and philosophy. There is no difference in principle, Hayek argued, between the economic philosophy of Nazism, socialism, communism, and fascism and that of the American welfare state and regulated economy.

Americans were outraged. "How can you say that we are against freedom and free enterprise when our soldiers are fighting and dying against the Nazis on the battlefield?" Americans asked. They forgot that the communists, who themselves were not paragons of liberty, were also dying on the battlefield against the Nazis. "How can you say we are against freedom and free enterprise when the Roosevelt administration engaged in a massive governmental intervention into the economy to save free enterprise?" Americans asked. It was the intervention itself—and the collectivist philosophy that guided the intervention—that was the problem, Hayek said. One does not save freedom by destroying freedom. Hayek warned Americans that if they continued following this road—the road to the welfare state and the regulated economy—they would end up with an Americanized version of communist Russia, Nazi Germany, and fascist Italy.

Proponents of the welfare state vilified Hayek and others who repeated the warning. We can travel this road, they said—the road to the New Deal, the Great Society, the welfare state, and the managed economy—without any bad consequences, as long as we call this way of life "freedom" and "free enterprise."

Thus, decade after decade, through taxes and regulations, governments at all levels took ever-increasing control over people's lives, wealth, and property. The control grew exponentially, decade after decade. The rationale was that the control was necessary—for society, for the poor, for the nation, even for freedom itself. Americans continued living their life of the lie: They continued believing that the more control government exercised over their lives and property, the freer they became.

This is the mind-set that has been created in public schools throughout most of the twentieth century. It is not a coincidence that the overwhelming majority of the American people support the core philosophy of the welfare state: that what ultimately matters is not the sovereignty and freedom of the individual but rather the sovereignty and control of the government. It is not a coincidence that Americans overwhelmingly support what our nineteenth-century ancestors rejected: public schooling, income taxation, Social Security, Medicare, Medicaid, farm subsidies, and so forth.

Having been forced to pledge allegiance and to listen to government-approved schoolteachers for twelve long years, the minds of the American people have been molded well. Good citizenship means: Praise America's "free-enterprise system"; obey the rules; don't question the authorities; monitor and turn in your fellow citizens; and support your public officials, especially in times of emergencies. And all in the name of freedom and free enterprise.

Fortunately, thousands of us have broken free of this government-molded mind-set. And this is what separates us from our fellow Americans. They are still trapped within the prisons of the mind that were erected through years of political indoctrination. We have broken free of the walls our schoolteachers, knowingly or unknowingly, erected around our minds.

How is this division manifested in society? All of us feel the deep pain associated with the losses in Oklahoma City. But Americans who are still trapped by the indoctrinated mind cannot fathom why the rest of us feel the same pain, anger, and outrage over the deaths of the Branch Davidians in Waco, Texas, and of the Weaver family in Ruby Ridge, Idaho. We weep over those deaths as much as the deaths in Oklahoma City. And we ask uncomfortable questions, such as: Why didn't their funerals receive the same public attention and presidential appearance as those in Oklahoma?

Unlike the majority of our fellow Americans, we know that the U.S. government did travel the road to collectivism that Hayek warned us about fifty years ago. We recognize the welfare state for what it is: a program of massive political stealing labeled as "free enterprise"—backed up by the iron fist of the Internal Revenue Service. We see the war on poverty and the war on drugs for what they are—wars against the American people—brutal wars that are resulting in death, destruction, and impoverishment every single month. We know that such agencies as the IRS, the CIA, the FBI, and the Pentagon have deliberately killed, tortured, and terrorized innocent Americans.

But many Americans cannot yet see this. They cannot bring themselves to face the horrible truth: that their own government has become an organization of state terrorism. They accept that foreign governments—the Soviet Union, China, Rwanda, Mexico, Argentina, and so forth—engage in murder and terror against their own citizens. But the reality that this is where the road to serfdom has brought the United States is still too nightmarish for the average American to accept. His mind simply will not assimilate and process the data.

The commissioner of the Internal Revenue Service recently appeared on television and said that America's income-tax system was voluntary. The average American nodded his head and said, "She's right. I'm glad I don't live under communism, where taxation is involuntary." The rest of us immediately saw the commissioner's statement for the lie it was. Every day, IRS agents levy liens on homes, bank accounts, and businesses; they confiscate cars, furniture, boats, and other personal property without the constitutional protections of notice, hearing, and due process. If a person forcibly resists, government agents kill him for "resisting arrest."

Or take the war on drugs. The average American says, "The war on drugs has been beneficial." The rest of us see reality. This war has destroyed thousands of Americans. It is also a pretext for government agents to rob innocent people in airports and on the highways—they seize and confiscate large amounts of cash and say to their victims: "Sue us if you don't like it." And more and more judges, politicians, intelligence agents, and law-enforcement officers are on the take—as dependent on the drug-war largess as the drug lords themselves.

Yes, there are two mind-sets in America—one that sees the U.S. government's failed wars as "freedom" and "free enterprise"—and the other that sees them for the evil and tyranny that they are.

The cancer that threatens our body politic is the life of the lie— the life of the indoctrinated mind—that still afflicts our fellow Americans. Herein lies the reason that, while they can feel anger and outrage over Oklahoma City, they are totally befuddled over the anger and outrage that we also feel over Waco and Ruby Ridge. Our fellow Americans oppose private and foreign-government terrorism with all of their hearts. But they cannot yet bring themselves to recognize and oppose the public terrorism that their own government is engaged in.

Did the U.S. government engage in murder or manslaughter at Waco and Ruby Ridge? The evidence is convincing. (See Chapter 9.)

But President Clinton says that the Branch Davidians instead killed themselves. How does he arrive at this conclusion? Clinton told the accused killers and terrorists—Attorney General Janet Reno, the BATF, and the FBI—to investigate themselves. Their report: "Mr. President, we investigated, and we determined that we did nothing wrong."

Suppose the federal judge in Oklahoma says to Mr. McVeigh: "Sir, I want you to investigate whether you have done anything wrong." Mr. McVeigh returns to court and says, "Your honor, I investigated, and I determined that I did nothing wrong." Would you be happy if the judge released him? Would you say that justice had been done?

The situation is similar to the instances when Adolf Hitler would receive a report that the Gestapo was abusing the German citizenry. He would order Gestapo leaders to investigate the matter. They would return with: "My Führer, we investigated, and we determined that we did nothing wrong." Hitler would reassure the German people.

The core issue facing the American people is this: Have the guardians become the terrorists? If they have, then isn't it rational for people to fear the guardians—*especially when their congressional representatives themselves fear ordering an independent investigation into Waco and Ruby Ridge?* (It is difficult for congressmen and presidents to forget the threats of former FBI director J. Edgar Hoover: Don't mess with the FBI, or we will disclose the files we have on you.)

Isn't it rational for Americans across the country to arm themselves and to unite in large groups—just in case they themselves become the guardians' next target? If the guardians have become the murderers, and if elected representatives will do nothing about it, then what are the people supposed to do—permit themselves to be killed or forcibly defend themselves?

In Nazi Germany, the guardians became the murderers. But German public officials, including schoolteachers, repeatedly said: "Good citizenship means obedience to law and order." Those who spoke out were called unpatriotic troublemakers—they were monitored by the Gestapo for counterterrorist propensities. The Jew was considered a model citizen because he obeyed the law by going to the gas chambers without resistance. When a small number of Jews forcibly resisted arrest—by shooting back at the police—Hitler and

German officials were outraged. "The law is the law. How dare you violate it?"

But Americans are different from the German Jews. They come from a long history of resistance to tyranny. Americans will not be killed—they will not permit their wives and children and friends and neighbors to be killed—without resistance. Americans may go down at the hands of their guardians, but they will go down fighting.

If government officials did, in fact, murder our fellow Americans at Waco and Ruby Ridge, does this mean that individuals had a right to exact revenge by bombing the federal building in Oklahoma City? No! One has the right to defend himself when the guardians become the murderers. But self-defense when one is under attack is different from killing government officials when one is not under attack. For once, President Clinton was right: It is evil for terrorists to kill innocent people—whether at Oklahoma City, Waco, or Ruby Ridge.

Unfortunately, President Clinton refuses to focus on the government's own wrongdoing. Instead, he blames the Oklahoma City bombing on talk-show hosts and critics of government misconduct who have had the courage to expose the wrongdoing. Rather than end the government's wrongful conduct, the president wants it kept quiet.

The president—and the American people—must ultimately face an uncomfortable fact: The terroristic conduct of the U.S. government—both foreign and domestic—has produced thousands of potential terrorists all over the world who have a reason to exact revenge against the United States.

The best way to end private terrorism is to end the U.S. government's public terrorism. This would mean the end of both foreign and domestic wars, including the wars on poverty, drugs, and guns, that the U.S. government has waged for most of this century. And it would mean the dismantling, not the reform, of such terroristic agencies as the BATF, the DEA, the CIA, and the IRS.

This essay originally appeared in the June 1995 issue of Freedom Daily, *published by The Future of Freedom Foundation.*

13

The Oklahoma Tragedy and the Mass Media

by Richard M. Ebeling

The hundreds of pictures and thousands of words that have appeared in the popular press since the Oklahoma City bombing tell us much about America and its people. The images and descriptions of the killed and wounded have aroused the sympathy and concern of millions of Americans. Countless prayers have been offered for the dead and those they left behind, and charitable contributions have been sent from every corner of the country to assist in the wake of a terrible human tragedy. Once again, Americans have shown themselves to be a generous and caring people, in the tradition that has been the hallmark of all previous generations since the founding of the nation.

In those pictures and words, however, has emerged another side of contemporary America. It has to do with how many reporters, opinion makers, intellectuals, and political analysts see America, because those numerous stories about various aspects of the Oklahoma tragedy have not only contained the facts of the case and the surrounding circumstances, but interpretations, as well, that have given the facts a particular shade and color. In other words, these molders of public opinion have attempted to convince us of what the Oklahoma tragedy is supposed to mean in terms of American politics and culture.

With few exceptions, the mass media and popular press generally have had one interpretive narrative running through all the stories and commentaries: America is threatened by a minority of "right-wing" extremists who preach hate for and fear of the U.S. government; this minority is obsessed with a desire to arm itself to the teeth with all types of weaponry and is forming itself into citizen militias that pose a danger all across the land; this minority is linked to or influenced by racist and neo-Nazi organizations; and even when these groups outwardly disown violence, their rhetoric and arguments are the feeding ground for creating "crazies" who are willing to commit terrorist acts against the government and innocent people.

The uniformity of this interpretation demonstrates just how much the mass media and how many in the intellectual community are out of step with what is actually going on in America and how influenced they are by the "spin" given to events in the briefings and handouts supplied by various government agencies. The reporters, intellectuals, and political analysts who dominate that mass media basically buy into the "party line" of the government establishment.

But what else can one expect? After all, they went through the same propaganda mill of state education from kindergarten to graduate school. They all tend to look upon the state as the benevolent redistributor of wealth and the caring social engineer who will remove the blemishes of an unjust market society. They all tend to view themselves as the educated elite who see and know so much more than the average middle-class American who populates that vast wasteland that separates New York from San Francisco.

Let us look at some of their misunderstandings of the Oklahoma tragedy.

Who is responsible? Typical of the collectivist mentality and its corollary of collective guilt, the mass media immediately picked up on President Clinton's theme that it was not the actual bomber who was responsible for the act of terrorism in Oklahoma City. No, it was the purveyors of hate and anger on talk radio and the Internet, whose sick conception of the government made the perpetrator do it. He could not help himself—the evil hatemongers made him do it. To admit that the perpetrator had acted on the basis of his own free will would mean that he was responsible for his actions and their consequences. This is too much for the collectivists in our midst, who have cultivated the ideology of a "nation of victims," to accept. Without this ideological anchor, what would be left of their aging rationales for redistribution and social safety nets and the political power that comes with these government policies?

Who are these hatemongers, with their antigovernment paranoia? According to *Time* (May 8, 1995), "Most are not violent people, and many of them have understandable grievances about feeling left behind in the economic competition of the 1990s." Yes, even many of the hatemongers and paranoids who made the perpetrator do it are themselves victims, according to the thinking of those in the mass media. They are supposedly the latest victims of capitalism; these are the people who lost their jobs when heartless corporations moved jobs overseas in search of cheap labor. They feel resentful as the benevolent state tries to compensate for the injustices of the past through humane affirmative-action policies. And in search of "simplistic" answers to "complex" problems, these "simple people" encapsulate all their frustrations in the government, which has let them down.

That many of the people who have expressed concern and fear of the government have done so because the state has increasingly threatened or suppressed various individual freedoms is apparently beyond the understanding of the enlightened scribes of the mass media. To take seriously the ordinary American's perspective might undermine their idyllic fantasy of the paternalistic state—a state that knows what is good for the people better than the people themselves.

What freedoms have been lost or threatened that drives these "extremists" and "paranoids"? The establishment press has enumerated the concerns about liberties that many of these Americans are fearful of losing. In the Western states, there has emerged a growing movement in opposition to the encroachment of the federal government over land use, water rights, and government's abrogation of the private title to property in the name of "environmental protection." State and local governments have lost their traditional authority to an overpowerful and overbearing Washington. Tax burdens confiscate the income and wealth of those who have earned it in the marketplace; the Federal Reserve System possesses an unlimited authority to print paper money in any quantity deemed desirable by the monetary central planners. The taxing and money-monopoly powers of the federal government, therefore, threaten the economic well-being of every American.

Federal agencies such as the Bureau of Alcohol, Tobacco and Firearms run roughshod over the rights of the citizenry, the cruelest and most brutal example being the massacre of the Branch Davidians at Waco, Texas, in April 1993. Even one of the members of the jury at the Branch Davidian trial following the massacre said afterwards: "The federal government was absolutely out of control there. We spoke in the jury room about the fact that the wrong people were on trial, that it should have been the ones that planned the raid and orchestrated it and insisted on carrying out this plan who should have been on trial." (For one of the best articles on the federal siege, attack, and destruction of the Branch Davidian compound and the perverse trial and sentencing of some of the survivors, see "Waco: A Massacre and Its Aftermath" by Dean M. Kelley, *First Things*, May 1995.) Those who have chosen to arm themselves and train in the proper use of weaponry have concluded that the greatest danger to their life and property may come from "out-of-control" federal agencies that seem to stand outside the law and appear to be answerable to no one except themselves.

But in the eyes of the establishment press, these are "macho males" wanting to "play war games" in battle fatigues on weekends. The vast majority of those who report and write analyses for the mass media cannot understand why the "progressive" functions, responsibilities, and powers of the government cause such consternation among a growing number of Americans. Their articles ooze with sneering sarcasm and ridicule. Viewing themselves as enlightened moderns, they do not even realize that they are dominated in their own thinking by that thousand-times-refuted socialist idea that private property rights can be abolished or significantly diminished with no loss of personal rights and civil liberties.

But all rights ultimately arise from private property rights and can be retained in the long run only when they are respected and protected. And the first of these property rights is the right of self-ownership and the corollary right of self-defense, regardless of whether the aggressor is another individual or the state.

What is "right-wing" extremism? What makes someone "right-wing" in the eyes of the establishment press? From the descriptions offered in the mass media, a "right-winger" advocates strict constitutional constraints on the powers of the government; believes in the federalist principle of a division of powers among the national, state, and local levels of government, with primary decision making at the local level because it is closest to the people's control; holds that individuals should be secure in their lives, papers, and property from arbitrary searches and seizures; and considers that individuals should be self-responsible for the economic well-being of their families and the moral education of their children. And what makes someone a right-wing "extremist"? An extremist is anyone who actually takes these ideas seriously, believing that they represent the foundation of any free society and are worth defending.

The mass media tries to muddy the waters by saying that many of these "right-wing extremist" groups are connected with or influenced by racist, neo-Nazi, or fascist "radical extremists." The attempt to lump together strict constitutionalist individualism with neo-Nazism or fascism just shows how much those who write for the establishment press are still trapped in the Stalinist thinking of the 1930s, when the communist political lexicon declared that fascism was the extreme, last line of defense of capitalism and only the "progressive left" led by communists represented truth and goodness.

Who is the fascist? Individualism and the political philosophy of limited government is not only inconsistent with but is the exact opposite of fascism and Nazism. Under fascism and Nazism, the state reigns supreme with absolute power over everyone and all forms of property. It can well be asked: Who is the fascist, when the president of the United States and many Democrats and Republicans in Congress call for expanded authority for the FBI and other federal security agencies to intrude into the lives of the American citizenry? Who is the fascist, when the call is made for increased power for the FBI to undertake "roving wiretapping" or have easier access to the telephone and credit-card records of the general population? Who is the fascist, when the proposal is made to make it easier for the FBI to investigate and infiltrate any political organization or association because the government views it as a potential terrorist danger?

Who is the fascist, when it is proposed that a foreign resident or visitor in the United States should be open to deportation without a full disclosure of the supposed terrorist evidence against him? Who is the fascist, when it is proposed that the president should have the discretion to decide what foreign organization or association is peaceful or potentially violent and, therefore, whether Americans shall be permitted to voluntarily donate to it?

Who is the fascist, when it is suggested that perhaps shortwave transmission licenses should be revoked because some in the government or on the political left do not like what others say in their exercise of free speech? Who is the fascist, when the critics of "right-wing extremism" hint that perhaps the government might have to regulate the Internet, because the critics do not like the ideas that others choose to share among themselves?

Where do we go from here? The deaths in the Oklahoma City bombing were indeed a tragedy for America. That tragedy, however, will only be compounded if we allow ourselves to be taken down the road of even more government powers and controls because of the rhetorical and ideological biases that still dominate political and mass-media discourse in the United States. We have reached this point in America because of the distance we have already traveled down that road. Let us, instead, retrace our steps and find the road of freedom once again. We need a society in which everyone is safe and secure in his personal liberty, private property, and in his voluntary and peaceful associations with his fellow men. In the end, that more than anything else would heal the hurt, diminish the fear, and remove the anger that is causing divisions in our country. And the tragedies of both Waco and Oklahoma City could then pass into history, remaining only as lessons for us to remember and to learn from.

This essay originally appeared in the June 1995 issue of Freedom Daily, *published by The Future of Freedom Foundation.*

14

The Hypocritical War on Terrorism

by James Bovard

President Clinton is continuing to agitate for new powers to suppress terrorists. He is demanding more powers for wiretaps, more powers to prevent people from using encryption for their e-mail, more powers to classify normal crimes as terrorist offenses, and so forth. As usual, Clinton's solution to every problem is more power for himself and his cronies. Clinton has scorned opponents of his terrorist proposals, claiming that they want to "turn America into a safe house for terrorists."

It is difficult to understand how politicians can denounce any private opposition to increased federal power when the government is already rampaging in many areas of the nation. The drug war has resulted in a pervasive use of National Guard units for oppressive search-and-destroy missions against suspected marijuana growers in many states. Using the military for law-enforcement purposes is very effective, since soldiers are more efficient than regular police because they often openly scorn the Fourth Amendment and other constitutional rights.

It is important to recognize the hypocrisy of government officials regarding illegal actions that result in the deaths of many civilians. In the days after the Oklahoma City bombing, the Clinton administration launched a full-court press to whitewash federal action at Waco. When a journalist stated in April 1995 on Cable Network News that he considered the 1993 Waco federal attack a terrorist act, Labor Secretary Robert Reich rushed to distinguish between what the feds did at Waco and the bombing at Oklahoma City: "We are talking about acts of violence that are not sanctioned by the government—that are not official." Reich sounded as if the government has a moral magic wand that can automatically absolve law-enforcement officials of any abuse, regardless of how many dead babies are left when the smoke clears. Atrocities committed by the government cannot really be considered to be atrocities—instead, they are merely policy errors—or, more accurately, public-relations mistakes.

Clinton, in the days after the Oklahoma City bombing, called for Americans to "all be careful about the kind of language that we use and the kind of incendiary talk we have." Yet it was federal officials who demonized the "cult members" at Waco long before the feds themselves were demonized over their actions at Waco. At the 1994 trial of the Davidian survivors, federal prosecutors compared David Koresh to Hitler and Stalin and declared that the eleven defendants "are as much religious terrorists as the people who blew up the barracks in Lebanon, the people who blew up the World Trade Center in New York and Pan Am 103." Yet, four ATF agents stated after the raid that federal agents may have fired first at the Davidians at the original 1993 raid. The government's vilification of the defendants was rejected by the jury and contributed to the perception that the government, like some right-wing zealots, was fanatical about Waco.

Neither the BATF nor the FBI ever made any efforts to apologize for their abuses at Waco. Indeed, the BATF last year rehired two agents (with back pay) who had been fired for lying about whether they knew that Koresh was expecting the initial BATF raid. And no one should forget that, before the embers of the dead children had a chance to cool at Waco, BATF officials raced in and proudly planted their flag atop the smoldering ruins.

The Clinton administration's attitude towards terrorism—massive, deadly force used against innocent civilians—was epitomized at the House Waco hearings in the summer of 1995. The highlight of Attorney General Janet Reno's eight hours of testimony on August 1, 1995, was her revelation that the 54-ton tank that smashed through the Davidian compound should not be considered a military vehicle—instead, it was just "like a good rent-a-car." Apparently the

Justice Department had purchased the damage waiver and didn't worry about getting a few scratches or blood stains on those tanks.

Such an observation by Reno does not inspire confidence in the Justice Department's moderation in its future operations. The news media fawned all over Reno for her testimony and almost all the journalists failed to report Reno's "rent-a-car" comment. Yet, this comment goes to the heart of why Waco continues to outrage millions of Americans. The federal government used military force against American women and children—and then tried to cover up its violence and to pooh-pooh any critics. What are a few 54-ton tanks smashing into a home and gassing children among friends, anyhow?

Further evidence of the political abuse of the terrorist issue comes from comments by FBI Director Louis Freeh in 1995. Freeh repeatedly portrayed the new wiretap powers as vital in the fight against terrorism. But a report by the Administrative Office of the United States Courts in May revealed that the FBI and other federal agencies have dismally failed to use existing legal authority against domestic terrorist groups. Though the federal and state governments imposed a record number of wiretaps in 1994 (1,154), not a single wiretap was installed in the pursuit of arsonists, bombers, or gun-law violators. No such wiretap against alleged terrorists has been requested since 1988. The vast majority of wiretaps were targeted against drug and gambling criminals.

Further evidence of Clinton's hunger for more power is clear in his proposed antiterrorism bill. David Kopel and Joseph Olson recently observed in the *Oklahoma City Law Review*:

> The new terrorism bill defines virtually any crime as "terrorism," whether or not related to actual terrorism. "Terrorist" offenses are defined as follows: any assault with a dangerous weapon, assault causing serious bodily injury, or any killing, kidnapping, or maiming, or any unlawful destruction of property. Snapping someone's pencil, breaking someone's arm in a bar fight, threatening someone with a knife, or burning down an outhouse would all be considered "terrorist" offenses. Any attempt to perpetrate any of these terrorist crimes would be subject to the same punishment as a completed offense. Even a threat to commit the offense (e.g., "One of these days, I'm going to snap your pencil") is likewise labeled "terrorism." The extra federal power created by the legislation is superfluous to

genuine antiterrorism. It was already a serious federal felony to make a real terrorist threat, as by threatening to set off a bomb, or to assassinate the president.

Clinton and Democratic congressional candidates in 1996 made political hay over the fact that the Republicans had not kowtowed to this particular Clinton power-grab.

Clinton's proposed antiterrorism legislation also greatly expands federal wiretap authority. The Clinton administration wiretap legislation would allow the use of illegal wiretaps in federal court and would also allow "roving wiretaps"—covering a large number of pay phones in the hopes of catching some lawbreaker. There is widespread fear among both liberals and conservatives that the Clinton administration could use the new wiretap authority to go after vast numbers of critics of government policy who pose no threat of violence.

Clinton's proposed legislation would allow wiretaps against suspected violators of any federal law. Jamie Gorelick, a deputy assistant attorney general, fanned such flames on May 3, 1995, when she told House International Relations Committee that tax protesters could be one type of "criminal" targeted by the expanded wiretap authority. Democratic Rep. Robert Scott of Virginia, questioning Louis Freeh on the same subject, asked, "Where would you have drawn the line to differentiate that tax protester from any other person that's just mad about paying taxes? I mean, are you going to subject them all to wiretaps to find out?" Freeh responded, "No, we wouldn't have the resources to do that." Yet, since the antiterrorism legislation will greatly expand the FBI's resources, far more tax protesters could presumably be tapped in the future. Private-property advocates who denounce the abuses of the Fish and Wildlife Service could be another easy target for the expanded wiretap authority.

The Clinton administration also announced that it had issued a new interpretation of the guidelines under which the FBI surveils domestic political organizations. The revised guidelines will give the FBI a green light to infiltrate far more private groups and political organizations. Assistant Attorney General Gorelick told the Senate Judiciary Committee that even "without a reasonable indication of a crime, a preliminary indication can be undertaken" and "you could use informants and you could collect information, and then determine whether you have reasonable indication for a full-fledged investigation."

Freeh gave a most expansive definition of terrorism in a speech last year to the American Jewish Committee: "Terrorism is the work of people and groups seeking to further their causes through fear and intimidation." By this definition, vast numbers of cynical Americans—for instance, individuals who call talk radio shows and denounce government abuses—could be classified as terrorists. And the payments to all the potential informants could really drive up the old federal budget deficit.

And Freeh has been either manipulative or naive when he speaks of public concern about government abuses. Freeh declared on May 13, "To my amazement, there are voices that . . . claim repression by government—and fear of government. . . . Sadly, I am astounded at these developments, as I think most Americans are." Once again, Freeh implies that the only decent attitude any American should have toward his government is blind trust, if not blind adoration. It is especially ludicrous for an FBI chief to express amazement at people's fear of the government, when the FBI itself trampled many citizens' rights in the 1950s and 1960s with burglaries, illegal wiretaps, character assassination, and intimidation, and when the FBI has yet to admit any misconduct in the cold-blooded killing of Vicki Weaver.

Another example of politicians' hunger to increase federal power over terrorism comes from a bill by Rep. Charles Schumer to create new mandatory minimum prison penalties for alleged terrorists. Kopel and Olson noted:

Some of the new proposed mandatory minimums for "violent antigovernment extremists" would impose a two-year mandatory minimum on someone who shoved a policeman during an argument over a traffic ticket, a two-year mandatory minimum on a jilted teenage girl who sent her rival an anonymous letter "I'm going to tear your eyes out," and an eight-year mandatory minimum on a homeowner who waved a baseball bat at a zoning inspector.

As far as Oklahoma City goes—I am all in favor of the death penalty for the people who carried out that bombing. Certainly, there is no excuse for killing innocent human beings in the name of any principle of politics. But there is nothing that the Oklahoma City bomber(s) could have done that would have somehow ex post facto validated what the federal government did at Waco, as Treasury Secretary Robert Rubin implied before the 1995 Waco hearings. The crimes of private citizens cannot absolve the previous and future crimes of federal agents. It is important for critics of government to act responsibly, but it is important for the government to keep one thing in mind: We shall not be silenced.

This essay originally appeared in the December 1996 issue of Freedom Daily, *published by The Future of Freedom Foundation.*

About the Authors

James Bovard is the author of *Shakedown: How the Government Screws You from A to Z*; *Lost Rights: The Destruction of American Liberty*; *The Fair Trade Fraud*; and *The Farm Fiasco*. His articles appear regularly in the *Wall Street Journal*; *Playboy*; and the *American Spectator*.

Richard J. Davis is a dentist in Hurlock, Maryland.

Richard M. Ebeling is the Ludwig von Mises Professor of Economics at Hillsdale College, Hillsdale, Michigan, and serves as vice president of academic affairs for The Future of Freedom Foundation. Professor Ebeling and Jacob G. Hornberger are the co-editors of *The Dangers of Socialized Medicine*; *The Case for Free Trade and Open Immigration*; and *The Failure of America's Foreign Wars*.

John L. Egolf Jr. is a schooteacher in Monroeville, Alabama.

Jacob G. Hornberger is the founder and president of The Future of Freedom Foundation.

Benedict D. LaRosa is a historian and author residing in San Antonio, Texas.

Sheldon Richman is vice president of policy affairs for The Future of Freedom Foundation and the author of *Separating School & State: How to Liberate America's Families*.

Jarret Wollstein is a director of the International Society for Individual Liberty, 1800 Market Street, San Francisco, California 94102, and the co-author of two books: *The Rage of Islam* and *What Really Happens When They Confiscate Your Gold*.

*D*ivine providence has given to every individual the means of self defense.... To disarm the people ... [is] the best and most effectual way to enslave them.

—George Mason

About the Publisher

The Future of Freedom Foundation

Founded in 1989 and based in Fairfax, Virginia, The Future of Freedom Foundation is a 501(c)(3), tax-exempt, educational foundation. Its mission is to advance liberty and the libertarian philosophy by presenting an uncompromising moral, philosophical, and economic case for individual freedom and limited government. FFF's journal, *Freedom Daily* ($18 per year), is a monthly publication of libertarian essays.

FFF's uncompromising tradition is carried forward in its books and tapes. The books are: FFF's award-winning *Separating School & State: How to Liberate America's Families* by Sheldon Richman; and four books edited by Jacob G. Hornberger and Richard M. Ebeling: *The Dangers of Socialized Medicine*; *The Case for Free Trade and Open Immigration*; *The Failure of America's Foreign Wars*; and *The Tyranny of Gun Control*.

The Foundation neither solicits nor accepts government grants. Operations of The Foundation are primarily funded through subscriptions and donations.

The Future of Freedom Foundation
11350 Random Hills Road
Suite 800
Fairfax, VA 22030
Tel.: (703) 934-6101
Fax: (703) 352-8678
E-mail: 75200.1523@compuserve.com
Website: http://www.fff.org